A **LIFETIME** OF **MAMMALS**

A LIFETIME
OF MAMMALS

Derek Warren

Matador
9 Priory Business Park,
Wistow Road, Kibworth Beauchamp,
Leicestershire. LE8 0RX
Tel: 0116 279 2299
Email: books@troubador.co.uk
Web: www.troubador.co.uk/matador
Twitter: @matadorbooks

ISBN 978 1788036 177

British Library Cataloguing in Publication Data.
A catalogue record for this book is available from the British Library.

Printed and bound by CPI Group (UK) Ltd, Croydon, CR0 4YY
Typeset in 11pt Minion Pro by Troubador Publishing Ltd

Matador® is an imprint of Troubador Publishing Ltd

It is with sadness we find ourselves having to write this. Our husband, father and grandfather devoted a number of his latter years compiling this book and it was his wish to publish it.

Unfortunately, whilst he had finished his writings he passed away without seeing the completed works in print.

We hope you enjoy reading this as much as we know Derek enjoyed living, recalling and writing it.

Love always, your wife, son, daughter, and grandchildren. xx

.

Contents

Acknowledgments

My thanks are due to the many people who have freely given of their time with advice and helpful comments on the contents of my book. I would like to express thanks to my wife Margaret and my son Stephen for their help with the manuscript and contents. Ben, my grandson, also deserves thanks for his patience in advising me with the many ways of using the computer more effectively.

Special thanks for their help in reading the manuscript and offering helpful advice are due to my friend Adrian Middleton and Professor Judith Jesch of Nottingham University.

Thanks are also due to Richard Paget for suggesting this book and for many happy memories badger watching together in several counties, and at the sett near his home in South Yorkshire.

Many farmers and landowners allowed me access to their land and without their help I might not have been able to record in script and photographs the many happy hours I have spent in the company of badgers, foxes, deer and the other native mammals, as well as introduced species mentioned in the text.

Introduction

Mammals do not receive the same status as birds or botany from those interested in natural history and this is understandable since birds are easily seen during daylight hours, and nocturnal species such as owls and nightjars are easily seen when the locations are discovered, or shown by those experts who specialise in such birds. Lots of bodies represent the interest of birds such as the Royal Society for the Protection of Birds (RSPB) and the British Trust for Ornithology (BTO) as well as lots of locally based organisations such as the County Wildlife Trusts. There are also various county bird watching groups whose members watch and record the various bird species, keeping members informed of rarities can turn up on their web pages.

Botanists are also well catered for with such bodies as the Botanical Society of the British Isles, the Wildflower Society and the various interested groups within the County Wildlife Trusts.

Whilst certain specialist groups cater for badgers and deer, these are usually involved with the protection of the individual species, for example the Badger Trust, which caters for the welfare and protection of the badger and debates with government over, for example, the welfare and treatment of the animal where there is the problem of bovine tuberculosis (bTB) in cattle and wildlife species. The Deer Society as the name suggests is concerned with the welfare of deer of all species and is also involved with the control of deer numbers in the absence of large predators such as wolves and brown bears, alas sadly no longer with us.

Foxes also have people interested in their welfare and there is a National Fox Welfare Society and the Fox Project who give advice on treatment for sarcoptic mange and also advise on other aspects of fox welfare.

My own interests are mainly with British mammals especially the carnivores. I have spent a lifetime looking at badgers and foxes and the smaller mammals such as stoats, weasels and polecats, as well as rodents such as squirrels, voles and the various mouse species.

I have worked for a number of ecological consultancies mainly in the field of badger conservation and have also surveyed smaller mammals in a consultancy capacity. For many years I advised various local authorities on problems concerning wildlife law and assisted the Crown Prosecution Service and the RSPCA as an expert witness in many cases of illegal activity concerning wildlife, especially badgers.

I joined the Mammal Society in January 1965 and helped with the various surveys into the distribution of a number of mammal species including badgers and the smallest British mammal the harvest mouse. As a member I had an input with the early Protection of Badgers Act of 1973 along with other Society members, notably my late friend Richard Paget as mentioned in the section on badgers. I have learned a lot from the scientific members of the Society and their contributions are mentioned in various sections of the book. I have also an interest in all forms of wildlife and have kept animals including badgers and foxes that were injured or somehow handicapped until they were suitable for release. This book is written for those with an interest in wildlife and covers a range of British mammal species, those who wish to learn more about individual mammals are well catered for. There are a large number of books written by specialists in their field, many of these are included in the bibliography.

Badgers (*Meles meles*)

Introduction

The badger is probably the best –known animal of the British countryside with its striking head pattern making it easily recognisable. Pub signs often feature the head of a badger such as the one used at a pub near Annesley in Nottinghamshire known as the 'Badger Box'. According to a local paper answering a reader's question, the pub formerly called 'Robin Hood' got its name from Minnie the badger who was captured when a tunnel was being dug at Annesley Warren, the badger was caught and kept at the public house in a barrel and baited by dogs. The badger usually won and finally managed to escape and disappeared into the countryside.

There is also a brew known as Badger Beer, the bottle features a badger on the label. A badger's head is also used as the logo for the Wildlife Trusts. Parts of a badger were popularly used for sporrans, especially the head, and of course dorsal hair was used for making shaving brushes as well as expensive

paintbrushes used for stippling. There are many old country names for the badger, the most ancient of these is *brock;* this is Celtic in origin and is found in names such as Brockhampton in Gloucestershire, and Brockholes in South Yorkshire. Interestingly, there is a badger sett a few metres from the county road sign for Brockholes.

The badger we know either through watching the animal or reading about it, is well distributed throughout Europe and parts of Asia, and is known as the Eurasian badger *(Meles meles)*. Badgers are carnivores and belong to the family *Mustelidae* along with the other native carnivores the otter, stoat, weasel, polecat and pine marten. The introduced mink is also a member of this family.

Badgers are the largest carnivore in Britain weighing in at around 8.8kg in the summer months and increasing to around 12.2kg in the autumn when at their heaviest. Male badgers are usually heavier than the females by around a kilogram, the heavier weights in the autumn are accounted for by the animals feeding up on the increased food availability when large quantities of fat are stored under the skin. In severe weather during winter the animals are able to stay underground absorbing the fat layer, thus avoiding the need to search for food that may be scarce at that time of the year. The above weights refer to mature badgers; juveniles are of course much lighter according to age and sex.

The heaviest badger I have personally met with was one that sadly had to be destroyed for safety reasons; this was a boar which weighed an incredible 18.5kg. The post-mortem showed that this badger was healthy even though it had been showing signs of abnormal behaviour. It had taken up home under a wooden classroom at a boys' boarding school and some of the boarders had been poking sticks under the building and provoking the animal to appear in the open.

Because of the way the animal was reacting, my friend, Richard Paget, a conservation officer from the local Wildlife Trust, and myself, decided that the animal had almost certainly been kept in captivity and dumped nearby. It was therefore not suitable for rehabilitation so the inevitable conclusion was reached. Although a badger-friendly farmer who had a deserted sett on his land had travelled from Lincolnshire with suitable equipment to remove the animal, we thought that our decision was the right one, bearing in mind the aberrant way the badger was behaving.

Whilst at the boarding school, one of the masters told me that the Divinity Master had tried to take a photograph of the badger whilst following it at night in his pyjamas, along a footpath. The badger apparently took exception to being followed and turned on the master who fell backwards and held the badger at arms, length by the throat. The animal then took off, heading for the classroom under which it had taken up residence. Next day when hearing of the incident on the previous night, one of the boarders asked the master who had tried to photograph the badger if he thought God had created the incident in order to try to get him to swear?

Setts

Badgers are communal animals living together in a collection of tunnels and chambers usually interconnected, these are maintained by members of the colony and is known as a sett. Normally the underground tunnels of a sett are of a surprisingly uniform nature and are around 30cm in diameter. Side tunnels are often enlarged to make a chamber around a metre across. The chambers are used by the badgers for sleeping in and accommodate the sow and cubs during the breeding season. Entrances to setts are usually much wider than the underground tunnels and are often polished at the top and sides where the animals enter and leave on a regular basis. When the animals are digging underground, earth is deposited at the entrances, and over a time this can make quite large mounds known as spoil heaps. Snuffle holes are probably made from inside the tunnel by a badger clawing upwards or by using its snout to push up to the surface. Once when visiting a sett in the late afternoon, I saw a snuffle hole lit by a shaft of sunlight. I could see into the tunnel and was surprised to see a badger lying with its head between its forelegs apparently enjoying the sun's rays. The badger continued to enjoy the sun for quite a while before the sun's rays fell away.

Badger setts are found in all kinds of locations from deciduous woodland to coniferous forests, hedgerows, disused quarries and watersides such as coastal areas, riverbanks, railway banks and canal sides. Usually sloping ground is preferred since it carries water and spoil away from the sett entrances. There are a number of recorded instances of setts being found on level ground at or below sea level.

Sometimes at a sett one can hear the animals moving about underground, especially around emergence time. On occasions the scraping of earth can be heard before the animals emerge backwards throwing soil they have scraped out behind them. They then repeat the process a number of times until they have achieved their task or have tired of the activity. Much digging seems to take place in the late autumn, possibly when the dominant sow is preparing a chamber to receive her cubs in the new season.

I well remember one occasion when watching badgers. I was sitting on the ground close to a sett entrance when a badger appeared above

ground, looked at me briefly and then disappeared below ground. After a few moments it reappeared backwards, dragging earth and scattering it between its hind legs, showering me with earth. The animal repeated the process several times, before tiring and moving off. I was then able to shake myself down and watch the night's proceedings. The badgers at this particular sett were habituated to my scent and I was able to watch them without interfering with their normal activities.

Setts vary in size and the number of entrances is not an indication of the number of animals in occupation. Single hole setts are usually outliers, that is a sett that is sometimes found within or at the extremity of the territory. Outliers may be occupied by a single animal that may be old and pushed out of the main sett, or used by a badger to drop in for a rest whilst out foraging before heading back to the main sett. A sett that was watched over a number of years by Adrian Middleton consisted of a single hole but contained a colony of badgers that at one time numbered around ten animals. In Whitwell Wood on the Nottinghamshire/Derbyshire border there is a large badger sett which had at one time some ninety entrances yet housed a colony of fewer than ten badgers.

One of the factors determining where badgers dig their setts seems to be the ease of digging into the ground. Badgers seem to be able to detect where there may be a bed of sand lying beneath a layer of clay. A sett near my home is located on a steep bank of sticky clay, nevertheless badgers have dug into the clay and in places have located a bed of sand and their diggings alternate between sandy and clay subsoil.

Some setts dug in sandy soil seem less stable than those dug in heavier types of earth. In the Strelley area of Nottingham I visited a wooded area where I was shown a sett dug in a very light sandy earth. The sett had been attacked by badger diggers and had been dug into by opening some of the tunnels and following them to where the animals were located. The tunnels were only about 30cm below ground level. This was easy digging and not surprisingly it appeared that all the badgers had been taken. By contrast, in heavier soils where badgers may have been attacked by badger diggers, the tunnels can be more than two metres below ground and can consist of a series of tunnels at differing levels.

For recording purposes, a number of categories have been used to describe different types of setts. Usually there are breeding setts, often the main sett where animals are in permanent occupation, and other setts where badgers may or may not be at home. These lesser-used setts may be used when there is an expansion in the number of animals within a territory, or be unoccupied, or used to a lesser extent, perhaps when numbers are depleted. They may also be used when an elderly animal gets evicted from the main sett or becomes less dominant, when for example a young boar moves into the colony and pushes out the once dominant boar.

Setts known as outliers are usually some distance from the main sett, often at the edge of the territory. A territory is an area used by a colony of badgers and usually contains all the requirements of the animals. An ideal territory would consist of deciduous woodland bordered by grazed pasture with a stream or pond nearby.

Outlying setts are sometimes used by badgers for breeding. A friend told me that he had observed at a single-hole sett a young sow badger and her cub.

Outliers may also be used when animals are feeding some way from the main sett and in these cases they may be occupied for a few days or perhaps only a few hours during the night when the animal may become tired or perhaps need to digest food before setting off home or continuing foraging.

In Derbyshire near Cheedale there is a limestone cave housing a colony of badgers. There are no excavations as spoil and the walls of the narrow v-shaped entrance are highly polished by the animals entering or leaving the sett indicating a long occupancy. In the entrance to this very active sett there are a number of latrines, usually these are small scrapes containing faeces near the sett or on the territorial boundaries. In this case the entrance to the cave was covered with large piles of faeces.

I discovered a similar cave sett in a steep escarpment above the River Lynn near Lynmouth in Devon whilst holidaying in the area. Like the Derbyshire cave sett it had a single entrance which was well polished, again there were no excavations. The badgers may have been living in natural cavities in the limestone with no loose material to take outside. Setts that have more than a single entrance (sometimes called a blind hole) are nearly always interconnected underground. Reports of setts that have been excavated after the badgers have been excluded invariably show this. In one licensed operation with which I was involved, the sett had to be destroyed once the badgers had been excluded. This provided a good opportunity to study the sett layout. All the underground tunnels were carefully exposed by a skilled operator and were found to be interconnected. The degree of expertise shown by the operator in this case was impressive.

A similar incident described by my late friend Bill Cunnington, where a sett removal was required for a road construction in Leicestershire. Bill was acting as an expert advising during the operation. After the badgers had been excluded for two weeks, the sett was carefully opened up, only to find a badger still in residence. It had retreated to the very end of the last tunnel about to be destroyed. The animal was ushered out and went off to find a new refuge within familiar territory. The badger in this case was indeed fortunate to be rescued otherwise it might well have starved to death underground.

The careful opening of a sett where this is deemed necessary should only be undertaken by a skilled digger-operator, a badger expert ought to be present in case any animals remain underground. As well as the examples quoted above, other cases are recorded where a sett has been fitted with one-way gates to allow the animals to leave the sett and prevent them from re-entering. After two weeks the sett was opened only to find one or more animals remaining underground.

Sometimes setts become deserted and are unused for a long time, perhaps permanently. Why is this? Some form of interference, such as illegal digging, may have taken place destroying the integrity of the underground chambers and tunnels, causing the animals to abandon the sett. In two cases I have been involved with, setts had been deserted because they were illegally gassed, perhaps killing badgers underground. In one of these cases it was known that a gamekeeper had put Cymag (a cyanide substance now banned) into the sett entrances allegedly to kill rabbits; however, a thriving rabbit warren nearby was untouched.

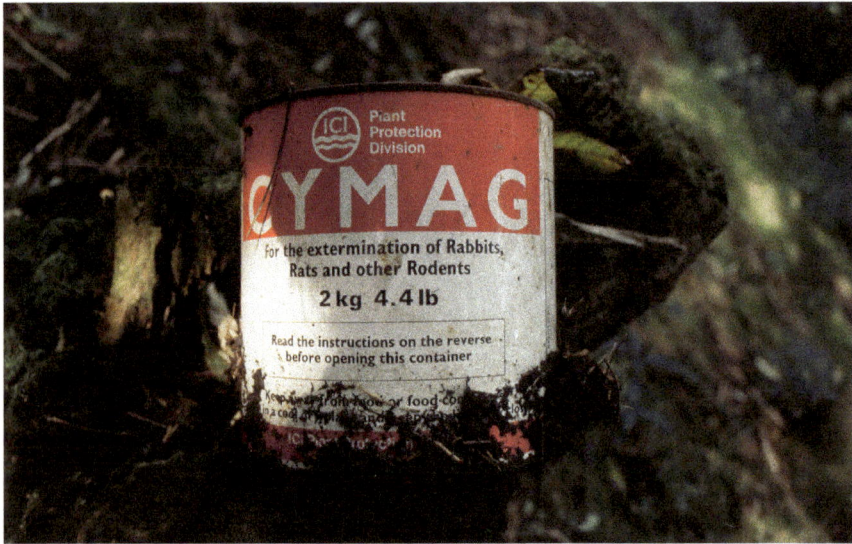

A sett in South Yorkshire was situated in an old quarry rented by my late friend Richard because of his interest in the badger. This was a main breeding sett producing a family of cubs most years. In some years foxes also used part of the sett not used by badgers to rear a family of cubs.

This sett remained active for many years and was situated close to a large arable field bisected by a thorn hedge. The badgers used to cross the arable field using a well-worn pathway alongside the hedgerow to visit another sett in woodland around 1000 metres away. No doubt badgers from the woodland sett would also use the hedgerow path to visit the quarry sett on occasions.

Eventually the hedgerow was removed and consequently the badger path running alongside it was destroyed. Not having the cover of the hedgerow and the path ploughed up, the badgers would have felt exposed, crossing what became a massive open space devoid of cover. They ceased their nightly wanderings and sadly the sett became deserted as it is to this day.

Ancient coal pits such as the day holes found in parts of South Yorkshire where coal was dug out by the light of day are occupied as setts. The entrances to these long disused day holes have collapsed and badgers have moved in, living successfully there. The interesting thing is that when the badgers emerge from the coal workings, the white on their faces seems remarkably clean considering they are living in a former coal pit.

Other man-made situations such as drainage pipes when dry are sometimes taken over by badgers. One such pipe near my home measures approximately eighty metres in length and 30cm in diameter, and is occasionally occupied by badgers. One year the pipe housed a sow with cubs at one end of the pipe and at other end there was a vixen with cubs. I managed to get photographs of the fox cubs by lying in the ditch at the end of the pipe used by the foxes. Unfortunately the end of the pipe used by the badgers was in a steeper part of the ditch and was too difficult to negotiate.

One day a dog walker in the village was passing this pipe when he heard whimpering sounds coming from the end of the pipe housing the badgers, thinking this noise might be from a trapped dog, he called the RSPCA out. I heard of the incident and went to investigate and was able to explain to the attending officers who were about to break open the pipe, that the sounds emanating from the pipe were those of badger cubs and not a trapped dog. Fortunately my advice was listened to and the result was no damage to the pipe and the badgers were left in peace. Whilst typing this piece I checked the pipe and was delighted to find evidence of badgers occupying the pipe and foxes were using the other end of the pipe exactly as described in the previous paragraph.

An incident of illegal digging where there were badger cubs present was investigated by me some years ago, when a main sett was attacked by badger diggers and the sett was seriously damaged, the badgers moved out for a while. Eventually I managed to trace the badgers: they had taken refuge under a garden shed using the facilities provided by the previous residents, a family of foxes, may have been evicted by the badgers. People living nearby told me that the earth/sett had for many years, been used by foxes and the badgers were newcomers. Whilst there I knelt down and placing my head near the entrance to the underground refuge I was able to hear the whimpering of badger cubs below ground. Some months later I checked the main sett and the badgers had returned; they had cleaned out the sett and were digging fresh tunnels.

The temporary sett under the shed then became disused, no doubt the foxes would reclaim it in the next breeding season. The diggers had damaged the main sett and almost certainly took some of the badgers. They were successfully prosecuted and substantial penalties were imposed.

Many years ago a group of badger enthusiasts attended a Mammal Society meeting at Ironbridge in Shropshire. We were there to look at local badger setts. We crossed the famous Iron Bridge and on a steep wooded bankside we were shown some small rectangular concrete tunnels associated with the long disused iron works. These tunnels were used in the past to carry cables or heating underground and they had been taken over by badgers, and were now polished at the entrances where the badgers had entered and exited over many years.

Artificial fox earths built in woodlands to ensure a breeding population of foxes, were common in the heyday of hunting. Although some more recent artificial earths have been constructed, the remains of most of the more ancient ones have fallen into disrepair. Whilst carrying out survey work in woodlands in the north of Nottinghamshire I saw a number of these earths. In some local woods there are several such old artificial earths, some of which are now occupied by badgers. When badgers occupy man-made constructions such as pipes or artificial fox earths, these are for legal reasons classed as badger setts. The Protection of Badgers Act 1992 defines a badger sett as "any structure or place indicating current use by a badger".

Many badger groups now construct artificial setts to receive orphaned animals or as alternative accommodation where a natural

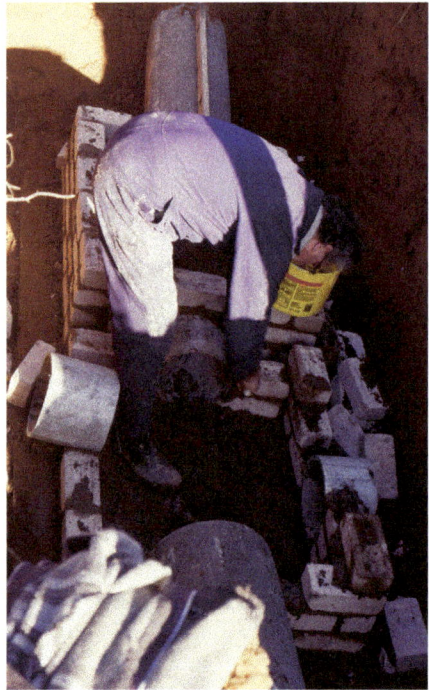

sett may have to be closed down because of a road building programme or some other reason. I have been involved with the construction of artificial setts and with sett closure where the animals had been excluded before a sett was destroyed. Providing the animals are properly housed and the habitat is suitable, artificial setts can be successful. One such sett in a neighbouring parish I advised on more than twenty years ago still has a thriving colony of badgers today.

Badgers have on occasions been known to sleep above ground, usually in the summer months. I have seen a pile of hay stored inside the bole of an old hollow tree where a badger had been resting. On other occasions whilst visiting setts during the daytime I have several times seen badgers emerge from a cornfield and enter the sett, these animals had been sleeping above ground. A cornfield, once fully grown, would to a badger or other animals appear as a miniature forest, offering cover and relative quiet until perhaps rain storms or harvest time.

Rarely, badgers will construct a nest above ground and Ernest Neal in one of his books records such a nest containing a sow badger with cubs. This nest was constructed in a dense hedgerow. A local man was passing the hedgerow when he noticed the nest and poked his walking stick into it whereupon a sow badger jumped from the nest and made off. A subsequent investigation revealed the presence of cubs.

Once whilst holidaying in Scotland, in the Cairngorms, I went to look at a sett situated in woodland near Aviemore. It was late afternoon and I was fortunate to see three badger cubs playing with the remains of a rabbit. One cub would seize the rabbit and make off with it whilst the other cubs gave chase, then another of the cubs would snatch it back. This went on for several minutes before they gave up the game and wandered off. I went to watch the sett the following night and noticed the rabbit carcass was still lying nearby. Making myself comfortable to watch the badgers, I was amazed when a buzzard came down and was about to pick up the rabbit when it noticed me sitting there and hastily took off, minus the rabbit.

Packing away my camera after the badgers had dispersed, I became aware of a pinging sound coming from behind me. I was aware of shapes in the darkness all around me and peering into the woods I could see that I was surrounded by deer browsing, I then realized that the pinging sound I had heard was the hind legs of the deer catching the wire fence as they leapt into the woods. The deer eventually drifted away into the night leaving me with some rewarding sightings.

On another occasion after driving to the next village one freezing February morning to pick up the Sunday papers. I returned at around 11am by way of a different route, passing a large badger sett situated on a steep bank-side. Glancing up I was astonished to see a badger standing in the snow looking down at the road. Minutes from home I returned with a camera hoping to capture a rare picture but sadly for me the badger had left the scene. I wondered why the animal would be out in the morning in such inclement conditions.

Badger paths are tracks made by the animals leaving the sett area and moving towards the regular feeding areas or to other setts within a territory. These pathways become well worn even down to the bare earth, and show up particularly well where the animals regularly cross roads or ditches. Such paths are very distinctive when crossing meadows or moorland, are often used by other animals including man and are sometimes used as territory markers between neighbouring social groups.

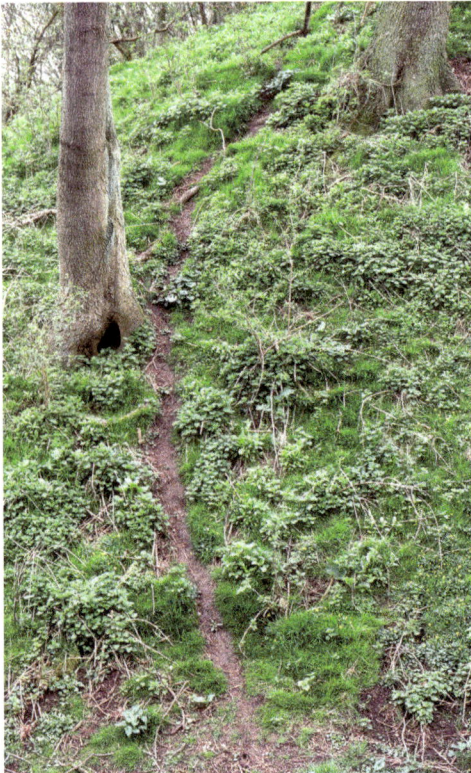

Badgers, when they walk, place their feet side by side and register their five toes on soft earth thus leaving a track about the width of their body. Even when the print is incomplete and only shows two or three toes these are easily recognised as badger since the toes are almost in a straight line. Foxes walk placing one foot in front of the other rather like a cat and leave a narrow track.

Once on holiday in Ireland I was able to locate a badger sett by following a roadside track back across a pasture for about a quarter of a mile to the sett situated in woodland.

Badgers take bedding underground especially during the summer and autumn months when there is a plentiful supply of dry leaves, hay, bracken or other suitable material. The animals gather the bedding by raking the leaves, or whatever material is available into a pile then tucking it under the chin, or in the case of a large bundle beneath the body before dragging it backwards with a shuffling motion towards the sett entrance. The process of taking the bedding backwards without looking is achieved by the animals squatting and leaving a drop of scent when setting off to collect bedding, then having collected bedding, following the scent trail back from the bedding source to the sett. In other words the animals are able to travel backwards with their bedding without looking. I was once told by a gamekeeper that when he wanted to catch a badger he would wait for a badger to go off collecting bedding, then once the badger was engaged with its task, he would creep forward and put a sack in the sett entrance. The returning badger would drag the bundle of bedding into the sack whereupon the keeper would spring forward and pull a drawstring thus trapping the badger. This was long before legislation protecting badgers.

Having watched the badgers collecting bedding at a local sett, I persuaded a local farmer to leave a bale of straw at harvest time in the field near the sett. The badgers within a few days had usually taken the whole bale underground. The bale mentioned was the old rectangular type. Another farmer friend used to leave one of the huge round bales of straw near his sett. It took a whole season before all the straw was taken underground. There would be long trails of straw leading from the edge of the wood where the bale was delivered, to the entrances of the sett where individual animals had taken their supply of bedding underground.

Badgers seem reluctant to take anything into the sett other than bedding. However, ramsons (wild garlic) and other aromatic plants are sometimes taken below ground. Ramsons give off a very strong smell, especially when trodden upon or crushed, as would happen when being dragged underground. One wonders why an animal with such a sensitive sense of smell would tolerate such a powerful aroma in the underground tunnels of the sett. It has been suggested that some of the strong smelling material collected as bedding, such as ramsons, may have an affect on the parasites which inhabit all occupied setts and the animals themselves.

Very small cubs will on occasions try to gather bedding. I remember seeing a very young cub probably above ground for no more than a few nights trying to collect a few wisps of grass lying around the sett entrances and struggling to take it below ground.

Occasionally, during a dry spell, badgers will bring out piles of bedding and leave it outside the sett to air for a night or two before taking it in

again. I have seen this happen on several occasions at a sett near my home, especially during a dry spell in the winter months. There would be little fresh bedding available at this time of the year so existing supplies would be recycled. Bedding is broken up through wear and tear during underground activities and can often be seen in the spoil as fragments brought out with the earth when fresh digging is taking place.

Feeding

Badgers are omnivorous and will eat whatever type of food is available at a particular time of the year. In Britain earthworms are eaten in great numbers when available, which is on mild wet nights when worms of several species come above ground to feed and mate and are easily taken by the badgers. The animals seize the earthworms by the head and slurp them up at a prodigious rate. I was able to observe this behaviour closely when a badger came to stay with us for a few months as described below. Sometimes more earthworms are eaten than can be digested and I have on a number of occasions seen and photographed, near a sett, piles of worms which have been regurgitated, and which apart from one or two bites at the head end appear complete and undigested. At another sett situated within a large collection of bramble bushes, where seasonally masses of blackberries were immediately available, heaps of undigested blackberries were regurgitated around the sett area. The large surplus of available food was clearly too good to miss for the colony and, like children at a party, they appeared to have overeaten with the inevitable consequences. Locals had observed badgers climbing on top of the sprawling bramble bushes when the fruits were ripe at this sett.

In the early 1970s I, along with others, supplied the late Dr Keith Bradbury with fresh dung samples for work he was carrying out on badger diet. Keith was a pathologist at Leeds University and was interested in badgers as well as their feeding behaviour. The reports from Keith showed how varied the diet of the badger is. Earthworms were found in many samples. Fruit such as apples (possibly cultivated varieties) and blackberries were found in others. Surprising amounts of vegetable matter were also found. Fairly substantial amounts of grass and clover in some samples indicated they had been selected deliberately whilst on other occasions they appear to have been eaten incidentally along with earthworms. Elder bark was sometimes eaten, once flower petals were identified, possibly Calendula, a garden flower. The remains of various beetles and caterpillars were also found.

Cereals are eaten when available. Setts close to arable land enable the badgers to take advantage of the oats or wheat in the late summer months. After harvesting badgers will also go gleaning for spilled grain on the cleared land this seems to pass through the gut undigested as revealed in the contents of the dung pits.

Once whilst watching badgers on the edge of a corn field, a badger walked past me and went into the growing corn, whereupon it began swiping at the ears of corn, and, using its claws, drew the ears through its teeth, and with a chattering sound stripped the wheat from the stalk and devoured it. I have on other occasions whilst standing on the edge of the crop watched badgers taking the corn from the ground where it has fallen.

Post harvest, for a short time, provides a bonanza for small mammals and birds. Raptors, such as kestrels, sparrowhawks and buzzards, also move in on the newly revealed habitat picking off the exposed small mammals and birds.

Occasionally badgers will catch and eat small mammals such as voles and mice, and I well remember seeing a badger chase, catch and eat a

bank vole. Along with a friend I was sitting above a linear sett with several entrances emerging onto a well-worn pathway. We watched as a bank vole was scuttling around on the path right below us. Suddenly a badger emerged to our left and immediately ran towards the vole, seized it and, with a crunching of bones clearly audible to us, ate it.

Badgers will also eat carrion as well as more usual dietary items. Along with foxes they will clean up the remains of wood pigeons or pheasants after a shoot when some birds remain uncollected. One shooter I know leaves several pigeons on the ground especially for the foxes and badgers when he has finished for the day. In a similar situation, rabbit carcasses are sometimes left out for scavengers by ferreters, when they are too small or not wanted for the pot. I have been out with a ferreter who invariably left unwanted rabbits or their remains to be scavenged by badgers or foxes.

An animal when dead becomes carrion available to any animal that scavenges. Larger animals that may have been killed in a road accident, for example a fox or a badger, may be avoided as carrion for some time until decomposition sets in and the strong body scents have disappeared.

During a severe spell of wintry weather some years ago I took the body of a road casualty badger and placed it not too far away from a local badger sett, intending to retrieve the skull when the animal had decomposed. After a few weeks when I thought it would be about time to collect the skull I was surprised to see badger tracks in the deep snow leading from the sett to the remains of the badger. The animals had been eating the carcass, the remains were of course still badger, but without the scent of the animal they were simply carrion.

Breeding

Badgers mate at any time of the year but the main period of sexual activity takes place during the winter months, especially in February, when the majority of cubs are born. Mature sows come into season after giving birth and are mated. After mating sows have what is referred to as a period of delayed implantation, a small group of cells known as a blastocyst is formed in the uterus. No development takes place until around late winter when the blastocyst is embedded in the wall of the uterus and the gestation period begins. Young unmated sows may come into season at any time of the year and are mated. As in the older animals, a blastocyst is formed, which after a shorter period of delayed implantation results in the birth of cubs around the same time as the more mature animals are giving birth.

However, the period of delayed implantation in the badger can vary through stress or other environmental factors. It has been reported that a sow badger once taken to London Zoo was kept confined, then after some twelve months produced a single cub. From this it was considered that the gestation period of the badger was around twelve months. Through the studies of Dr Ernest Neal and others we now know much more about delayed implantation in the badger, which also occurs in other *mustelids* such as the stoat, but does not occur in its close relative the weasel.

Matings can last a considerable time. Once when I arrived at a large sett at Speyside in Scotland just after dusk, I could hear the excited whickering sound of a boar badger and using the weak light of a torch I could just make out the shape of a pair of badgers, which were paired and mating. By carefully creeping along the top of the sett I was able to take a photograph without disturbing the animals. I was there for around three quarters of an hour and the animals were still paired when I quietly retreated.

The number of cubs born to a sow seems to vary according to the type of sett and the quality of suitable habitat nearby. One sett situated on an old Ice House and surrounded by arable land of some 300 acres is bordered by mixed woodland on three sides. There are grass strips separating the woodlands from the agricultural land. The strips of grass are around ten metres wide and are part of an agri-environment scheme. The badgers at this sett produced on average three cubs per year. Another sett regularly watched was situated in a hedgerow bordered by arable land. The badgers at this sett had to travel some considerable distance to forage on grassland and in adjacent woods and as a result produced only one or two cubs per annum. A pair of cubs usually appeared above ground, others perhaps did not survive to make it above ground.

Orphaned badger cubs are often reared by specialised animal hospitals but in two cases in my experience orphaned cubs have been successfully reared at the sett without the animals being removed. These were badger cubs and were close to being weaned but still taking milk from their dam.

In May 2008 whilst away in Dorset I received a telephone call from my daughter Nicola who was driving near one of my local setts when she noticed a badger lying by the roadside. The animal appeared to have been hit and killed by a vehicle. On checking she saw it was a lactating sow badger and was able to let me know this. I was fairly certain I knew where the animal had come from and rang a friend Tom with the news and asked if he would check the sett and put down some feed.

Tom started feeding that night with a mix of liquid and solid food in plastic trays. I rang Tom the next day and was delighted to hear that the food was being eaten and the cubs were dragging the food trays into the sett entrances. The feeding was continued for several weeks and three cubs were successfully reared. When watching the sett later in the year I was delighted to see that two of the cubs were erythristic (ginger-coloured) and I was able to take photographs of these animals.

I had in the 1960s located a sett with erythristic badgers at a site in south Nottinghamshire. The sett when I became aware of it was in dense vegetation and in order to examine it I had to carefully cut a way into the sett area. The heart of the sett was in a small grassy clearing and after a number of visits I was able to confirm that all the badgers in this colony were erythristics. I was able to take photographs of some of the animals. These badgers became habituated to my presence and would groom and socialise whilst totally ignoring me, even though I was just metres away. If I took a friend then the badgers would resume their usual cautious behaviour because of unfamiliar scent associated with the stranger.

Some years after I located this sett a normal-coloured boar moved in and in subsequent years the erythristic colouring became diluted after he would have mated with the dominant sow. The badgers born after that were of a normal colour. (See Adrian's piece on colour variations at the back of the book).

An incident in north Nottinghamshire on the outskirts of a village was brought to my attention by the villagers.

They were seeing young cubs emerging from a broken pipe in a ditch. A lactating sow had been found dead by the roadside nearby. I advised that a feeding programme should be set up; this was arranged by local people who every evening fed the cubs with various canned dog foods. I was pleased to receive a telephone call some weeks later informing me that the cubs were weaned and were being seen playing. Artificial feeding was stopped and the cubs were seen later in the evenings behaving normally playing near the pipe in the ditch.

Another incident concerned a badger cub that had apparently got lost during the night and was found by a dog walker early one morning curled up fast asleep in a hedgerow. The dog walker took the badger cub home and telephoned the local police station and they then rang me for help. I collected the cub that seemed fit and took it home where it was fed, and during the night it became very lively.

On checking my records I found that there was a sett which was no more than 200 metres from where the cub was found and the next day I took it to the area of the sett, putting it down on a badger path. The cub appeared to know where it was and became excited. Once released it immediately ran

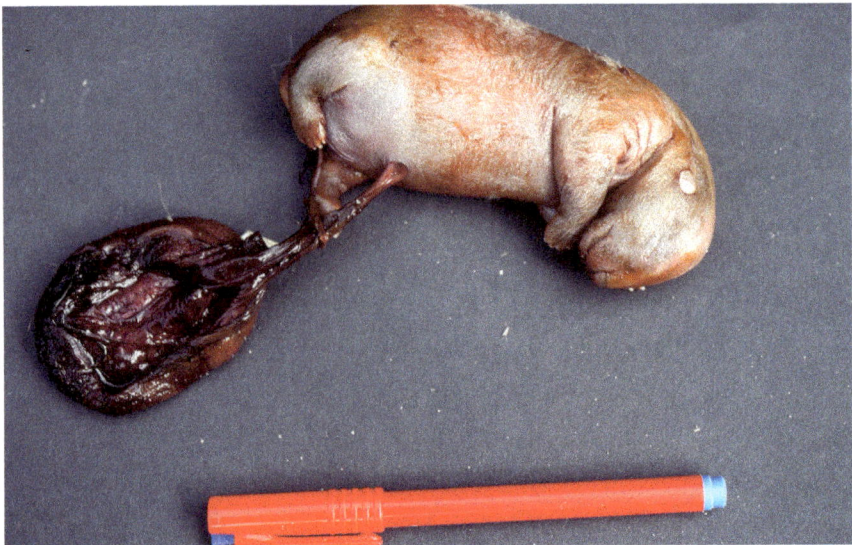

along the path and went straight into the main entrance of the sett. This was a relief as I knew I had the right animal at the right location. To introduce a badger to a wrong location could result in a sorry story for the strange animal in these circumstances.

Over many years I have taken badgers back to the sett area where they have been found caught in a snare or hurt in some way. They clearly know when they are being returned to their own area as they become very excited when they can smell familiar surroundings.

Television producer David Cobham asked me to act as an adviser to a professional wildlife cameraman for the filming of badger cubs for a forthcoming children's television programme *Woof*. My task was to locate two setts with cubs for the filming and to supervise the feeding of peanuts on a nightly basis at both setts. Two suitable setts were located and fortunately both were in the same parish and only a mile or so apart. The help of the landowners at both setts was sought and they were enlisted to carry out the feeding, encouraging the badgers to emerge early and feed at the areas suitable for filming. Sacks of peanuts were delivered to both locations and feeding was carried out for several weeks before filming was to take place.

The preferred sett chosen for the filming was situated on a bank in a paddock and was considered to be more photographically pleasing than the reserve sett. This sett was well known to me as I had regularly watched and photographed the badgers there and had observed that the usual number of cubs appearing above ground was around six. The landowner had fed the animals for many years with high protein dog food (she was a dog breeder) and was delighted to have badgers on her land. Supplementary feeding seems to have helped in the high survival rate of cubs at this sett.

A photographic hide partially concealed by a large sycamore tree was built at the chosen sett and along with the regular feeding of a dry dog food,

peanuts were also fed on a nightly basis. The badgers at the reserve sett continued to be fed in case there was a mishap at the sett chosen for the filming.

After a period of a few weeks of being fed peanuts, the cubs were coming out earlier than the normal emergence time and because of the supplementary feed were becoming quite tame. The professional cameraman employed by the television company was notified when the weather was suitable and after travelling from Wales, was successful in obtaining the required footage at the first attempt.

Territories

Badgers mark out the boundaries of their territory using latrines, often known as dung pits, with faeces, urine and the deposits of scent from gland situated under the tail known as the subcaudal gland. At the heart of the territory is the main breeding sett, this is defended by the resident badgers, intruders being chased away.

Often dung pits are found near or close to, or even on the sett, as mentioned elsewhere, dung pits can also be found in tunnels underground.

Dung pits or latrines, as the name suggests, usually consist of small scrapes used for a few nights, new ones are then dug. Sometimes there are several dung pits close together in a regular latrine area. Occasionally, however, dung is deposited on the ground without digging a pit and can sometimes be seen on or near a sett and on feeding areas.

The extent of badger territories, in a prime area for the animals, was demonstrated by Hans Kruuk in his studies of badger territories in Wytham Woods in Oxfordshire 1978. Badgers were fed a mixture of peanuts laced with treacle, together with small coloured plastic pellets.

The plastic pellets are passed through the gut undigested and are excreted with the faeces in the dung pits. Each social group was fed the prepared concoction containing their own particular coloured pellets. One social group for example might have been given red pellets, others different colours. The dung pits were then checked for the various coloured pellets. The pellets of a specific colour, for example red, would be located in a dung pit, then a line would be drawn back from the dung pits to the sett where that colour had been fed. The extent of the individual territory was then revealed. These were remarkably delineated and, according to the mapping, accurately marked individual group territories.

Sometimes pellets of a colour not fed to that particular social group or clan would appear in the dung pits of that group. For example red pellets appeared in the dung pits of a group fed with yellow pellets. This may be because an animal, perhaps a boar visiting a sow on heat in a neighbouring social group, leaving his faeces in the dung pits of that group.

Not all dung is deposited on the surface. I have seen in a collapsed tunnel of a shallow sett on Malham Moor an area of dung pits along the length of the collapsed tunnel. This depositing of dung underground is probably because the animals were living on open moorland with no suitable cover nearby to shelter their activities. Coincidentally whilst watching at this sett with Richard Paget (co-author of *The Badgers of Yorkshire and Humberside*) we observed a vixen with cubs playing at one end of the sett whilst at the other end a family of badgers emerged.

Underground latrines were also observed at a sett in Leicestershire, destroyed once badgers had been excluded prior to road building being undertaken. During excavations dung had been found deposited in some chambers of the sett, the skeletal remains of cubs that had died underground were also found in other chambers.

The cubs may have perished because their mother might have been involved in a road accident or some other incident and was therefore unable to feed them or perhaps their feeding was poor and they died naturally. It is known that in seasons when feeding is limited, perhaps because a scarcity of normal food items, young animals may die before they are old enough to emerge above ground. It is recorded that around a third of cubs perish in their first year.

Badgers are the largest carnivore in Britain of the family *Mustelidae*. All the *mustelids* have a scent gland situated under the tail, which is used to mark other individuals in a family or social group and as a territory marker. In the case of the badger the scent glands are well developed and are also used to mark their territory and sett area. Badgers also have paired scent glands in the anus and these are said to give the badger its characteristic earthy smell, as well as being used in the marking of territorial ranges. When going on strange territory badgers will squat periodically and leave a drop of scent on the ground. Badgers also press their hindquarters on other members of the group usually after emergence and scent mark them. This scent marking helps them to reinforce a collective group scent, consequently animals not having this communal scenting would be chased away.

When badgers are startled they will emit a musky scent that is very

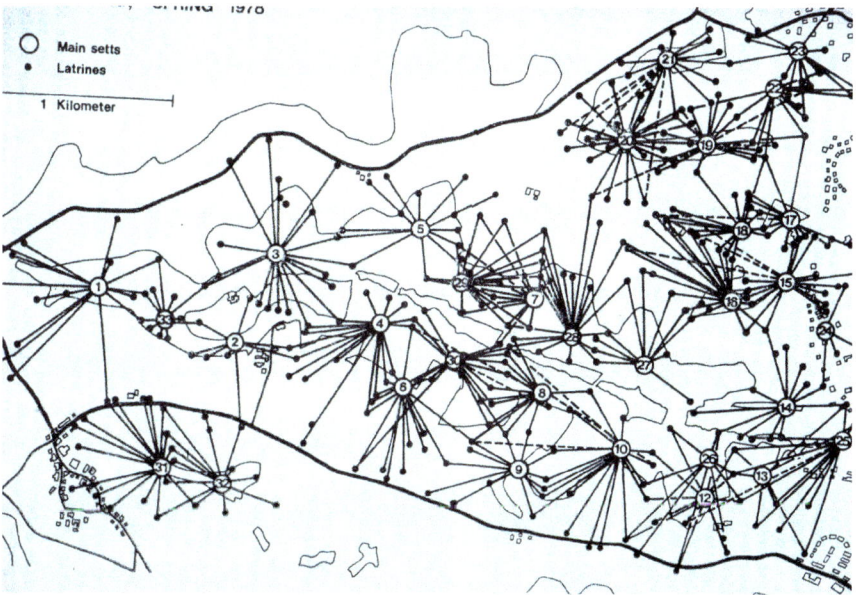

obvious to the intruder. Such scent can also be evident when cubs become excited during play sessions.

In the late 1960s Richard and I were invited to visit a house in a Derbyshire village where the owners kept a semi-tame boar badger in a stable, the owners were eager to try to reintroduce the badger into the wild and we were asked to help them to achieve this. We offered to try to find a deserted sett suitable for the animal. The owners were asked to have a crate made up for transporting the badger. This would be kept in the stable along with the badger to allow the animal to accept it. The badger was being fed with best quality dog food and prime cuts of beef.

We cautiously entered the stable for our first meeting with the animal who promptly sniffed our shoes and then squatted and deposited scent on them. The scenting was presumably either to accept us as honorary badgers or as part of the territory.

The badger was, we were told, in the habit of occasionally leaving the stable and wandering off as it was not strictly kept in, and was known to visit an active sett situated in an old stone quarry a few hundred metres away, sometimes staying away for a few nights. One day the owners, whilst leaving the house around midday, were astonished to see their badger being chased by another badger down the road and into the stable where it lived. Once in the stable, the door was closed and the other badger made off back towards the sett. Perhaps the chasing badger was another male animal and it was possibly dominant to the semi-captive badger.

In order to catch the badger it was tempted into the crate by a succulent piece of steak, the door was dropped and it was taken to the location of a deserted sett situated in a wood in South Yorkshire. The area had been previously checked for other setts and it was thought that the habitat contained a good mixture of feeding options such as grazed grassland and mixed woodlands. When the badger was first introduced to the unoccupied sett it was reluctant to enter and came out and made off along a pathway towards a road. Upon reaching the road it appeared to have lost its bearings and was running up and down the road. Richard and I had to wave down the oncoming traffic to prevent an accident and guide the animal onto the pathway back towards the woodland.

The flagged down motorists were quite surprised to see a badger running up and down the road pursued by two exhausted naturalists.

Eventually the badger seemed to find the path back to the wood and disappeared towards the sett where we had tried to introduce it. We hoped the badger would have settled in the new location or been accepted into another colony. This was in the 1960s and then there was little information on relocating badgers. Such a release would not be acceptable today as animals for relocation are kept in family groups and are required to be tested for disease before release.

Grooming

Badgers when first emerging will often have a good scratch using one of their back legs, or lay on their backs scratching their tummies with their forelegs. When approaching a sett one can sometimes hear scratching when a family is engaged in grooming activities. Often pairs of animals engage in mutual grooming where one badger nibbles the neck of the other whilst the nibbled badger grooms the other animal in a similar fashion.

Once when watching badgers in Scotland I had arrived rather late and the animals had left the sett and gone off to forage. Passing a barley field on my way back I could see a patch of the barley moving and realised that the badgers were feeding there. I was wearing an old overcoat and decided to see if I could lure the badgers out by imitating badgers scratching. Using my thumbnail I rapidly drew it up and down on my coat front giving a reasonable impression of a grooming session. Within a few seconds of doing this I was astonished to see the barley shaking as two badgers emerged in front of me. They looked at me and seeing they had been deceived re-entered the barley and carried on with their nocturnal activities. I tried rubbing my coat a second time but the badgers were not to be deceived again.

Sometimes there is a mutual grooming session when two animals, often the dominant boar and sow, nibble the neck of each other rather like horses do sometimes. This social grooming helps to cement the bond between individuals in a group or family.

Most grooming takes place during the spring and summer months when badgers emerge earlier in good light and have time to spare until dusk when it is safe to move on to the feeding areas. Badgers of course have their share of parasites and some of their scratching is due to the presence of fleas.

Relationships With Other Animals

Sometimes animals other than badgers can be seen emerging from an active badger sett. Rabbits are a good example. These animals are not living in the main chambers of the sett, they dig into the side passageways making tunnels matching their body size. Moles too, almost permanent underground dwellers behave similarly, making tunnels that match the size of their bodies. This enables them to feel their way around their interconnected network of tunnels in continuously dark conditions.

A friend and I once saw a cat enter a sett we were watching and after a while a badger emerged followed by the cat, then shortly afterwards another two badgers came out and moved away. On another occasion whilst watching a sett, we saw a man with a Jack Russell terrier pass by the sett on a bridleway. Suddenly the terrier ran away from his master and headed straight towards the sett and immediately dashed underground at the main entrance. The dog's owner was unaware of the dog's whereabouts and went on his way calling its name. After a short time the dog emerged and ran after its master, whereupon a badger appeared from the same entrance and started grooming. The badger emerged at almost the same time as the previous evening when I had also watched the sett. This showed that the dog and the badgers had probably not met underground.

Small dogs, particularly terrier types, are frequently found to enter badger setts and are sometimes reluctant to emerge in spite of the desperate owner's efforts in calling and offering food near the entrances. Usually the dog will emerge of its own accord if left for two or three days when hunger intervenes. The logic of this is that if the dog was able to negotiate the tunnels when it entered the sett it will be in a better position to exit when it has not eaten for a day or two. A rather different situation occurs when for instance a dog is sent underground to deliberately tackle a badger by diggers intent on locating the animal, digging it out for a baiting session or some other purpose. What happens when trained dogs are sent below ground will be discussed in another chapter.

A lady was out walking her dogs in a Nottinghamshire village in July 2009 on a public footpath next to an active badger sett. One of the dogs, a terrier type, took leave of its owner and bolted towards the sett, promptly disappearing underground. In spite of the owner's frantic efforts in trying to call the dog out it failed to appear. I was notified by the Badger Trust and attended the scene. Later on other agencies including Natural England and the RSPCA also attended.

Several suggestions were offered but the one of digging into the sett was vigorously opposed. It was eventually agreed that the most satisfactory course of action was to leave the dog to come out of its own accord. The owner decided to leave her car next to the sett with a door open as a familiar object for the dog to recognise should it appear during the hours of darkness. Frequent checks were made during the daytime to assess the situation. Three days later the dog was found to have emerged during the night and was lying on a seat in the car to the great delight of the owner who was re-united with her elderly pet.

The dog, ironically named Badger, was a Patterdale terrier, a breed sometimes used for tackling fox and badger especially when bred for this purpose. Interestingly, terrier type dogs not bred for this purpose make delightful pets. Ernest Neal kept a Jack Russell terrier of which he was extremely fond. (The Jack Russell terrier was originally bred by a hunting parson for flushing out foxes and consequently bears his name.)

An incident concerning a dog entering a badger sett was broadcast on a local television station. A lady walking her terrier dog through a local woodland nature reserve released the dog for a short time whereupon it

ran into the entrance of a large badger sett and disappeared underground. Although food and water were left near the sett entrance where the animal went to ground, food was probably taken by badgers and foxes. The water remained untouched probably because it was a mild spell and there would have been plenty of worms for both the foxes and badgers to feed on, worms are largely made up of water.

Eventually after a week the dog came out of the sett and was found by another dog walker apparently none the worse for its experience, except it was very thirsty and drank copiously from the water dish. There have been several incidents where dogs have been lost underground and the sett has been dug into and badly damaged, whereas in my opinion if the dog had been left for a few days it would very likely have come out of its own accord. After all if it could get down the tunnels it should be able to make it to the surface unless there has been a collapse in the tunnels underground or some other obstruction prevented this.

As mentioned earlier if the dog has been trained to harass badgers or foxes it will be reluctant to abandon the task it has been bred to carry out. In such cases injuries to the dog can occur and in some cases dogs can suffocate when buried with earth when badgers are trying to dig themselves in and away from the attacker/attackers.

I have spoken to a number of badger diggers when appearing as an expert witness for the prosecution at a number of court cases involving illegal badger digging and other offences. They have described instances to me as above. I have in my possession the skull from a Border terrier lost by badger diggers in a local sett. The digging was eye-witnessed by a man living rough in the woods nearby. Although illiterate he managed to scratch the registration number of their vehicle on a piece of rock. The diggers were well known locally and were later caught red-handed digging for badgers at another location. The dog skull mentioned was thrown out by badgers when cleaning out the sett some years later and is now in my possession. I knew one of the diggers and at one time the name of the dog was mentioned during a subsequent court case at which I was the expert witness for the prosecution, sadly with the passing of time I have forgotten the dog's name.

I once walked to a large sett situated on the banks of the River Soar in Leicestershire and met a man near the sett who told me that he often saw the badgers when he walked the fields at night with his dog. He was an insomniac and when unable to sleep he would take the dog for a walk. Several times whilst walking the fields in the early hours, the dog had met with a badger and the two animals chased each other around the fields. He said that there was no aggression between the animals and it was purely playfulness. For several years after I had first met him he would telephone me, often in the early hours, to let me know that he was out with his dog and it was playing with a badger.

Another incident concerning the relationship between dogs and badgers took place when we stayed in a cottage once owned by Beatrix Potter in the Lake District. The cottage was next to a farm, and wanting to locate some badger setts to watch, I contacted the farmer who offered to take me to a large sett on a neighbouring farm. We set off the next day to visit the farmer with the sett. Before visiting the sett we were invited into the kitchen for a drink and a chat about badgers. The farmer told us that he was once wary of badgers and slightly hostile towards the animal until one evening he opened his back door and was greeted by the sight of a badger feeding alongside his sheepdog from the same dish. He then started to put out the feed in the same spot in the yard on a regular basis and was delighted to see the badger feeding along with his dog on a nightly basis.

An amusing incident took place when I visited another Lakeland farmer and asked if he knew of any badger setts I could watch. He told me he had a sett on his land on a steep bank in one of his fields. We arranged to visit this sett and I took along my camera and flashgun hoping for a photograph. Travelling in his farm vehicle we arrived at a pasture field, we scaled the steep hillside until we arrived at a badger sett with a number of entrances, with spoil heaps spilling down the sloping land. I checked the entrances to select one I thought would be the most likely that the animals might appear, and set up my camera and flash. After a short wait a badger emerged and immediately ran up the hillside, it emerged so quickly I didn't have time to fire the camera.

The farmer turned to me and asked if I wanted a picture, I said I did, and with that he took off his jacket and stuffed it down the hole from which the badger had emerged, then started to chase after the badger up the steep hillside. I knew that he would have no chance of getting the badger to return to the sett and thought the whole thing highly amusing.

The red fox, a member of the dog family, sometimes uses part of a sett not currently used by the badgers to rear cubs. So long as the foxes keep their distance they are largely tolerated, however, should they stray too near the badger's area they may be chased away. Badger cubs have been recorded playing with fox cubs near setts. Very often adult foxes, especially vixens, sleep away from their cubs once they are active above ground and usually visit them in the evening to suckle them or, if weaned, to bring in a rabbit or other item of food.

I have on several occasions seen foxes emerge from a badger sett where they may seek refuge especially during inclement weather. Watching at a local sett over a few nights I regularly saw a fox emerge from a sett entrance and make off, however, on one occasion the fox emerged exactly at the same time as a badger from an opposite entrance, the badger grunted and darted at the fox which exited at breakneck speed!

Once watching badgers at a local woodland sett I could see in the adjacent grass field a family of fox cubs and a vixen playing close to the edge of the wood. A sow badger together with a single cub emerged from the sett and after a while started to move along a track just inside the wood towards the area where the foxes were playing. As they approached and were close to the foxes the sow uttered an almighty scream, the foxes disappeared, and the badgers came racing back to the sett and bolted underground.

I have only heard a badger scream on two other occasions. Once heard the scream cannot be forgotten, I could only describe it rather like the sustained squeal of a large pig objecting to being moved. In one area of Nottinghamshire where there are a number of active setts in woodland close to houses, residents have told me that on occasions they have been woken

in the night by blood – curdling screams followed by the noise of badgers fighting. Perhaps the screams are the result of territorial disputes between dominant animals, or may be distress calls of other animals witnessing the fighting. Whatever the reason it does seem that the screams seem to be associated with stressful situations.

Polecat ferrets have been known to appear from occupied badger setts. Adrian Middleton witnessed such an incident in the Yorkshire Wolds when one morning whilst looking at setts a polecat ferret appeared at the entrance. I also saw a ferret emerge from a badger sett during the daytime, someone rabbiting with ferrets may have lost the animal when it may have killed a rabbit underground and slept off the meal. The ferret would not have entered a chamber whilst a badger was lying there or it would almost certainly have been killed. As members of the *Mustelid* family ferrets are related to badgers and are a domesticated type of polecat. I once found the skull of a ferret outside this particular sett, the animal may have suffocated whilst underground or possibly been killed by a badger and the remains thrown out whilst digging.

Some Observations on Behaviour

Holidaying in Scotland in the Cairngorms many years ago I met up with one of Hans Kruuk's research assistants working with Highland badgers near Pityoulish. Paul Latour is a Canadian scientist who had previously worked with brown bears in his home country and was helping Hans with his work on the diet of highland and lowland badgers. Paul had trapped several badgers and fitted them with radio collars checking their location during the daytime, and at night followed them using an aerial receiver, each badger having its own frequency. Over several nights and days Paul invited me to accompany him when he followed the animals at night, checking their whereabouts and their feeding areas, and during the daytime checking the location of the animals and which setts they were sleeping in.

Following the collared badgers was interesting, and during dry periods we usually found the animals headed for the barley fields or were feeding on pig nuts (*Conopodium majus*) which grew profusely in the area. Paul was tall and had long legs and once he had located one of the collared badgers, set off at a pace I found difficult to keep up with. Negotiating barbed wire fences was not easy for me, mostly I had to go under the wire rather than over. On one occasion we walked straight into a badger, this animal was not wearing a collar, grunting, it speedily made off into the night.

During the daytime hours we checked the setts for individual signals and were surprised to find that, unlike the badgers I watched at my local setts, these animals moved around quite a lot. For example a badger I had watched emerging from one sett at night was found when checking the next day to be in a completely different sett some quarter of a mile away.

Another interesting observation of badger behaviour took place during a full moon when a group of Mammal Society members met up in Woodchester Park in Gloucestershire. We were stalking badgers that were fitted with radio collars and were carrying Beta lights which glow green in the dark. Dr Chris Cheeseman who was in charge of a programme investigating the problem of bovine tuberculosis in cattle and badgers, was our host and led us around the pastures using infrared binoculars looking for the collared animals moving around in the dark.

We entered a field with a wood alongside, the moonlight cast a shadow along one side of the wood. Using the infrared binoculars we picked up three badgers that were feeding just inside the shadowed area, the animals continued in a straight line alongside the wood avoiding the moonlit grassland. When the badgers reached the end of the shaded area they turned and made their way back still keeping within the shadow of the woodland. We were able to ascertain that none of these animals had been fitted with radio collars.

Sometimes badgers will bolt underground at the sound of a rabbit cracking a twig, yet will on other occasions totally ignore normally unfamiliar sounds or sights. Once, while watching a local sett situated in an old quarry during harvest time, I saw the badgers emerge at their normal time and stay on the sett area grooming and socialising whilst a large modern combine harvester was working the field above the sett, occasionally flashing the headlights over the sett and lighting up the badgers. The animals were able to ignore the noise and the flashing lights and bide their time until the work ceased, they were then able to leave the sett area and move on to the foraging grounds.

Once whilst watching a sett on a Bonfire Night when a large bonfire was lit in a garden near the sett, I saw the badgers emerge whilst the fire was blazing and fireworks were exploding all around. After an initial cautiousness the animals stayed on the sett area and involved themselves in grooming and other social activities until the celebrations were over and they could move off into the night.

When checking a local woodland sett on a spring afternoon, I looked down an almost vertical tunnel with a curve around a metre underground. I was amazed to see two cubs together. I was chewing a toffee sweet at the time and bit off a piece and dropped it into the tunnel, there was an excited chattering and a third cub appeared along with an adult badger I assumed was their mother. I continued to bite off small pieces of toffee from the two sweets I had left and dropped them into the entrance. I then quietly retreated and left the wood. This incident shows that badgers are sometimes active, often well before usual emergence times, especially young animals who are probably restless after a few hours sleep.

Badgers do some times appear sleepy even shortly after emergence. Ernest Neal told of a badger that had not long appeared above ground, falling into a deep sleep on a bed of hay it had raked together on the sett area, and slept for some time whilst he watched the other animals emerge and make off into the night.

The adaptability of badgers to unusual circumstances was clearly shown when a Shropshire farmer and great friend of the badger, the late George

Pearce, was made aware of animals living in a sett on a small island situated on a flood plain of the River Severn.

The setts became flooded in December 1993, the badgers were forced by circumstances to seek refuge from the flooded setts and to move to higher ground. Unfortunately for the badgers the whole area was under water and the animals were forced to climb small trees and shrubs such as elder to avoid drowning. George was able to photograph the badgers curled up fast asleep, several feet above ground in the trees.

When the floods subsided, the badgers were able to leave the aerial sleeping quarters and moved back to their old sett area. The original setts were too damp for the animals to use then so they dug a series of single-hole setts each occupied by each individual badger. When the main setts were completely dried out, the badgers vacated their temporary outlying setts, then cleaned out and reoccupied their original dwellings.

Badgers have always suffered from some form of persecution from man. Other animals generally avoid or ignore badgers perhaps because of their size as our largest carnivore. In recent historical times, they may have been attacked by larger carnivores, such as wolves and brown bears. Wolves existed in Britain until the eighteenth century, although the brown bear was exterminated probably as long ago as the ninth century.

Generally carnivores tolerate one another, attacking or killing other carnivores for territorial reasons rather than for food. For example the fox and the badger live cheek by jowl and are aware of each other on most nights, sometimes living very close together when for example a vixen may produce her cubs in a disused part of a badger sett. Man has been the main enemy of the badger for centuries and in spite of protective legislation they continue to be persecuted up to the present day. Recent evidence of illegal interference with badgers or their setts is not difficult to come by. In the case of farming many farmers are tolerant of the animals and I have farming friends who welcome them and in some cases actively encourage them onto their land by creating an area exclusively for them, even so far as building an artificial sett in the hope of attracting them.

On the other hand there are some landowners who discourage badgers and deliberately interfere with them or their setts. Two cases come to mind where land had changed hands and the new owners decided that the badgers were not welcome. The first instance was when a farmer bought some grassland and wanted to run pigs on the land. The ancient sett was on the perimeter of the land abutting a brook and apart from seasonal blocking by hunts was not interfered with. The new owner sought advice from an official source and was given rather unfortunate information suggesting he could deter the badgers by pouring cattle slurry into the sett entrances leaving one entrance open. Inevitably the badgers were buried in slurry, the sett was destroyed and remains inactive more than ten years later. The landowner was prosecuted and ironically the field where the sett was situated is now part of an environmental scheme and the landowner is being paid by the taxpayer to encourage wildlife on to the land.

The second instance concerns a small grass field close to intensively managed arable land. A deep ditch separated the grass field from the arable fields. In the corner of the arable land and by the side of the ditch there was a small but active breeding sett in a triangular area that could not be worked by machinery. The sett extended through a hedgerow and into the grass field. The badgers when digging would on occasions spoil into the ditch. The ditch at the sett area was invariably dry but in case of unusually heavy rain conditions I advised the farmer to drop some concrete pipes in the ditch near to the sett area to prevent the drainage being blocked. This was carried out and there were no subsequent problems.

Shortly after the drainage was sorted the badger-friendly farmer sold off the land concerned to an arable farmer, who immediately started removing the shrubs and semi-mature trees growing on and around the sett. I advised the new farmer that he would require a licence to carry out such work. A licence was obtained but it soon became obvious that no notice was being taken of the licence conditions and unlicensed work was still being carried out.

The drastic interference with the sett continued and the RSPCA attended and advice was given, even so, no notice was taken and eventually the police were asked to attend. I had taken photographs of the sett both before and during the illegal interference. When challenged about interference with the sett the farmer replied we had no proof of any interference to the sett. On being shown the photographs of the sett in pristine condition and those of the interference he realised he was culpable. He then claimed to have chased a fox into the sett when out hunting and therefore thought it was a fox earth.

Because of illness of one of those involved, the case never came to court. Fortunately for the badgers the land changed hands again and the sett and its inhabitants were received with interest by the new landowners.

Another instance of interference with badger setts took place in south Nottinghamshire when land changed hands and the woodlands were managed for intensive pheasant shooting. The previous landowner although a shooting and hunting man appeared friendly towards badgers and other wildlife, a large rookery in one of the woods thrived.

An anonymous letter was received by the Badger Trust indicating that two setts in the wood had been destroyed and the rookery had been shot out, In another wood owned by the same landowner the badger sett had been drastically interfered with and there was a dead badger in an entrance to the sett. I was asked to investigate the incident and together with a wildlife crime officer we checked the wood where the dead badger was reported, sure enough there was a dead badger in one of the sett entrances.

The badger was too decomposed to send for a post mortem examination. However, we found hen's eggs near to the sett entrances and some of these had many dead bluebottles surrounding them. The remains of the eggs were sent for analysis and were found to contain a poison identified as a banned substance lethal to mammals and other wildlife. A subsequent visit to the wood revealed three more dead badgers.

Shortly after this incident, beaters on a shoot in the same wood reported another dead badger, this was sent for post-mortem and was found to have an egg in its stomach. A search was made of premises used by keepers but no evidence of the poison could be found therefore whoever was responsible for the illegal activity escaped prosecution.

Other examples of the persecution of badgers occurred on a shooting estate in south Nottinghamshire when seven dead badgers were seen over a period of three weeks during the summer of 2010. The animals were found in and around the woods and rides, and on the grassland. They were too decomposed to send for post-mortem when found. It was therefore difficult to ascertain the causes of the deaths although it is extremely unlikely that they had died of natural causes.

Snaring

Snares are simply a loop of wire attached to a log or a peg in the ground and are set on pathways or gaps in hcdgcrows where animals regularly pass. Snaring although legal for foxes and rabbits does have to be free running and have a stop fitted to limit strangulation. Self-locking snares (snares that lock on as the animal struggles) are illegal although some free running snares are easily adapted to become self-locking. Snaring is well recorded as being inhumane and recommendations are often made for the abolition of their use. The Scott Henderson Committee as long ago as 1951 made a recommendation that snaring should be prohibited if practicable when looking at activities involving cruelty.

Snares are supposed to be checked at least once every twenty-four hours, however, in many of the instances I have witnessed this does not happen. Snares are not legal unless checked regularly, and many non-target species such as domestic pets and badgers are caught. In Sherwood Forest I once saw a fallow deer that had been caught by a hind leg in a snare that had to be put down by a ranger.

Sadly most of these cases are invariably found close to shooting estates or game rearing establishments. Foxes have no legal protection except under the cruelty legislation, and have been found snared locally with monofilament line, as used by fishermen.

A recent serious incident concerns a snared badger my wife noticed when travelling to the next village. I went to look at the animal lying on the roadway next to the grass verge. I took a photograph as I first observed the animal, which looked like a road traffic accident. A close examination revealed signs of snaring at the back of the neck, however, when I looked at the neck there was a deep cut severing the windpipe and an artery leaving a large amount of blood on the roadway.

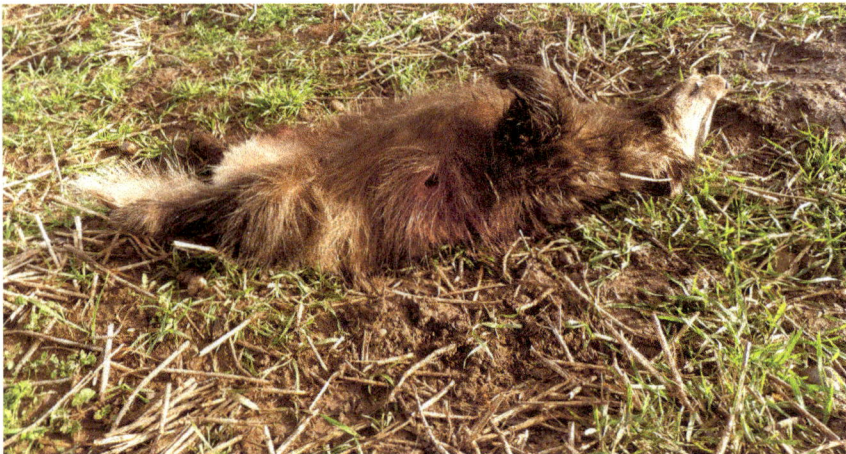

The badger, which was a lactating sow, was very emaciated and had, I believe, been taken from the snaring site to the roadside and either had its throat cut or the snare shaken to cause the fatal injuries. When I saw the animal it had not been there long as it was still bleeding when picked up. After I alerted the police and the RSPCA who visited the scene, the police officer noticed spots of blood leading back towards a gateway to a field, which housed feeders and pens relating to pheasant – rearing activities.

Some ten years before this latest incident the landowner had brought a live badger to me which was found snared in the same field containing the game rearing equipment. I was unable to remove the snare cutting into the neck of the animal. The badger was taken to a vet who removed the snare under anaesthetic. The badger was then taken to an animal hospital for a couple of days to recuperate. It was then brought back to the site where it was originally found and was successfully released back into the wild.

The dumping of badgers on the roadside after they have been snared or shot is not an uncommon practice. They are disposed of in this way to resemble a road traffic incident, the snares were probably removed before the animals were placed on the roadside. I have seen several such instances myself and always examine road casualties for injuries to the neck or for gun shot wounds before disposing of the carcasses.

Two badgers were found dead in the road near a large shooting estate in mid-Nottinghamshire by a police officer who became suspicious of the circumstances. One of the animals was taken to a local veterinary practice

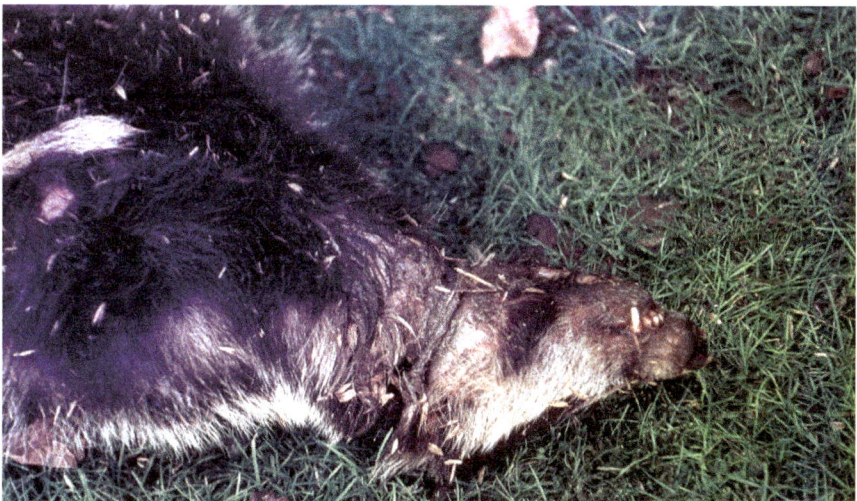

for examination and had been shot in the head. The police officer then returned to the scene and collected the second badger for a post-mortem, this animal had also been shot in the head. The badgers may have been snared and shot or were free on or near a sett when shot.

Another example of a badger being illegally shot occurred when a man living in a nearby village heard a commotion at the back of his house that bordered a pasture. The noise as described was a group of men calling, "Get in there!" and a lot of barking of dogs. Thinking that something was afoot the man rang the local police station and reported the incident, sadly the police said that they were unable to attend at that time and would take a statement the next morning which they did. Unfortunately no search was made of the area where incident took place. Although I was ill at the time and could not attend I asked David, a friend, to take my camera and check the field where the incident took place. When David checked the field he found, as I expected, a dead badger which had been baited by dogs, was in a bloody state and had a hole in its side where it had been shot. A shooting friend indicated to me that the weapon used was a twelve-bore shotgun fired at a close range, leaving a circular hole where the shot had penetrated the animal. David took photographs at the scene and also brought back the animal for me to take some pictures. I regret that I was unwell at the time and wished I had done more to investigate and perhaps had the unfortunate animal sent for post-mortem and the criminal activity properly investigated.

One Sunday morning I was checking a vulnerable sett along with my son when we became aware of some movement in the woods and were faced with a badger caught in a self-locking snare. The unfortunate animal had during the night wandered along a pathway near to a sett entrance and been caught in the snare. Having struggled all night the badger had managed to get the snare over its body and was caught around the pelvic bone. Whilst caught in the snare, the badger had been trying to dig itself in and there was a large circular area of bare earth. I took some photographs and went to the nearest farm to seek help in freeing the animal. The farmer came bringing with him a pair of cutters, which with some difficulty, he managed to cut the snare wire, allowing the badger to make its way back into the sett.

Earth Stopping

The practice of earth stopping or blocking of setts, earths, and entrances to open drains was commonplace before the Hunting Act of 2004. People known as earth-stoppers would act on behalf of hunts by blocking badger setts, earths, and drains, often the day before hunting or on the day of the hunt. Materials used as prescribed under the legislation would consist of a bag of untainted hay or straw or loose earth but often the methods and materials used were not as described in the act and a number of successful prosecutions took place. The purpose of earth stopping was to prevent foxes taking refuge underground when being pursued by hounds, and thus prolonging the chase. Foxes finding an open hole not blocked during a hunt would take refuge, then a terrier would be introduced to prevent the fox bolting and the animal would be dug out. The passing of the Hunting Act outlawed the blocking of badger setts and the Protection of Badgers Act 1992 was amended accordingly.

It had long been thought that badgers dug themselves out of blocked holes but this is contradicted by eye-witnessed accounts of badgers getting stuck in the entrances of blocked holes. I have myself watched a badger wriggling, trying to extricate itself from a blocked sett after hunt stopping. The badger I saw shortly after the sett had been blocked by an earth-stopper one Sunday morning, prior to a hunt in the area the next day, was forcing itself between the sides of the tunnel and the blockage. It would possibly have made off had it not seen me and fallen back into the sett entrance taking the collapsed earth with it. I photographed the badger lying in the tunnel where it remained, and was still there when I left the scene some twenty minutes later. I believe it is against the instinct of a badger to take earth into the sett. After all setts, when dug by a badger, are dug from the outside in and not the reverse. When setts are dug out under special licence where the occupants have been excluded, I have on numerous occasions examined the sett construction and have never seen loose soil within the confines of the tunnels and chambers.

I have been present when setts have been carefully excavated during a licensed operation after the badgers have been excluded and I have been impressed by the smoothness of the underground tunnels and chambers and the lack of loose earth or other debris, in other words the badgers when digging take out all the loose material which has been scratched from extending the underground labyrinth. The only material freely taken into the sett is bedding material.

My late friend Bill Cunnington of the Leicestershire Badger Group also confirmed to me an incident he reported in a letter to the *Melton Times* dated 14th November 2002 concerning a sett blocking by a Leicestershire Hunt. He had found a live badger trapped by clay and silt whilst trying to extricate itself from a blocked hole. The animal had been trying to exit an entrance by forcing itself between the side of the tunnel and the compacted material used by the earth stopper, and had become trapped round the pelvic area.

The animal was taken to a vet, who because of its poor condition had to put it down. A post-mortem was carried out and the animal was found to have a ruptured spleen and a distended bladder. The incident was shown to a Wildlife Crime Officer and photographs were taken. Another incident also in Leicestershire and told to me by Bill, was similar to the above incident but in this case the badger was dead when found, and must have spent many days trying to extricate itself by squeezing between the blockage and the tunnel walls before succumbing.

Unsympathetic earth stopping when legal must have caused considerable distress to animals hindered from exiting, or trying to enter a sett after the blocking. Many times I have seen setts heavily blocked by heavy clay, stones, wood and even a Cymag tin (Cymag was cyanide powder for use against foxes and rabbits but has also been used illegally against badgers. This substance is now banned for use against all species).

Much to my annoyance hunt earth stoppers have in the past trespassed onto private land to block setts using illegal methods. Several times I have tried to watch a local sett only to find the sett stopped and my evening ruined. Under the Badgers Act 1992 there have been a number of successful prosecutions concerning illegal methods of earth stopping.

After a number of illegal stopping incidents on a main breeding sett situated on a disused railway embankment in Leicestershire, a concealed camera was set up overlooking the main entrance to the sett which was situated in heavy clay. Before the hunt started an earth stopper was recorded on film, spading into the sett entrance seven large shovels full of the heavy clay, then stamping it into the sett entrance, thus making it

impossible for the animals to emerge. Other entrances were similarly dealt with. The camera recorded the illegal activity and the case was successfully prosecuted. The hunt was taken to task by the judge because the officials of the hunt were not present in court but left the earth stopper and the terrier man to carry the can.

Since time immemorial badgers have been dug out of their setts and subjected to all kinds of torture, from being maimed or disabled before being subjected to a baiting session, or simply being dug out of their setts, killed with a spade and put back into the excavation which is then filled in. Others bag the animals and take them to another location to have them at nearby site for prospective future digs.

In spite of being protected by strong legislation badgers are still being abused by people who take pleasure in locating and digging out the animals under the guise of so-called sport. Every type of dog from terrier to bulldog is used, the smaller type of dogs such as the terriers are used to locate the badgers underground, the larger dogs are used to attack the badgers when they have been dug out of the sett, or when they are taken away to be baited.

Terriers are fitted with a radio transmitter on their collars, and are urged to go underground with shouts of, "Get in there!" The animals are tracked underground using a hand receiver picking up the signals from the transmitter attached to the dog's collar. By listening to the strength of the signal on the receiver, which gives off a series of clicks, the depth of possible dig to be undertaken can be calculated. The underground activity is followed with the receiver until a fix is obtained, that is where the clicks are the loudest, and are not moving around. That is when the dog has located a badger and has cornered the animal in a chamber.

The purpose of the dog is not to fight with the badger but to keep it from digging itself in by nipping the back end of the animal thus preventing it from moving away or digging itself further into a chamber. Sometimes when the badger is frantically digging to escape the attention of a dog, the spoil can bury the dog and it can be suffocated. Badgers are not immune from being suffocated and badgers have been found in this condition when a sett has been opened up after an illegal dig. The animals are found with soil in their mouths and have died underground. I have been present and witnessed an incident where badgers have died in this way.

Not all dogs will enter a sett willingly; on one dig I covertly witnessed a terrier that would not go underground and was shaking, presumably because it may have suffered from being bitten by a badger or fox on a previous occasion. Another dog was substituted which did enter the sett willingly.

I have witnessed a number of illegal diggings into badger setts, one of the most blatant was in 1982 when my friend Bill Cunnington was travelling along the A6006 towards the Nottinghamshire village of Zouch. He happened to see along a hedgerow a number of men acting suspiciously and rang me to ask if I had records of a badger sett near there. This was on a Sunday morning and since I had visited the sett the previous Wednesday and taken photographs of its status I knew immediately where he was and I asked him to stay there unobserved and if possible keep an eye on the proceedings.

Having alerted the police who had been pre-warned of a possible dig, I drove to the area taking with me a camera and a telephoto lens. On my arrival Bill was waiting nearby observing the men. I started to take pictures of the men and their activity, we could see that one of the men was standing in a trench and digging and others were standing around with the dogs and checking other parts of the sett.

After a short time the police arrived and walked down the hedgerow which right angles to the road and arrested the culprits, collected the dogs and took them to the local police station where the three men were interviewed and statements were taken. One of the police officers

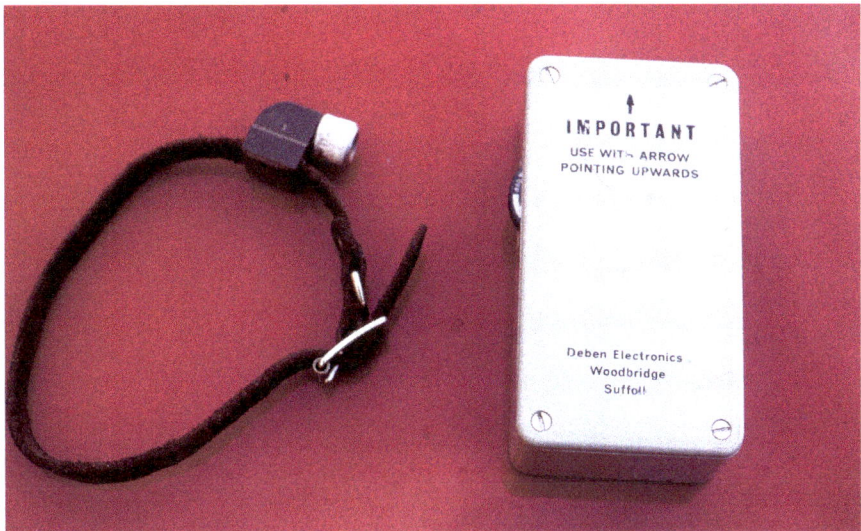

remembered seeing one of the men, when being approached at the sett, bend down near an entrance, and decided to return to the scene to see if this was of any significance. He searched the area and then decided to see if anything had been concealed in an entrance to the sett. Putting his hand into an entrance he pulled out a pair of metal tongs and returned with them to the police station.

One of the dogs had been injured during its time underground and the police suggested that it should be taken to a vet for treating as it would require stitches round the mouth. The men said they would deal with it themselves as the dogs received regular injuries from foxes and badgers.

The court case was heard in the Magistrates Court in Nottingham where Bill and I were the expert witnesses for the prosecution. One of the men decided to defend himself, he was a well known badger digger. Another of the defendants was employed by a local hunt as their fence and post-man (employed to repair fences damaged during the hunt). The chairman of the bench asked the accused who owned the badger tongs? All denied ownership, although the hunt servant said he had an identical pair at home. As a result of this admission all three accused were fined the maximum for having possession of badger tongs as well as being found guilty and fined for digging for badgers. All the equipment used during the dig at the sett was confiscated including the spades and tongs. The tongs were given to me after the case was concluded and were shown as an exhibit when I gave talks on badgers.

During the court case the accused produced photographs of the sett showing the smoothed over spoil heaps and fox prints leading towards the entrances. The fox prints had been made by pressing a fox's paw into the smoothed earth. Unfortunately for the diggers they had only used one right paw this was very obvious, making it look like the impossible trail of a one-legged fox.

Another case of the use of badger tongs was reported in the local press in 1972, before the first Badger Act of 1973. A family of badgers was living in the path

Chloe Warren

of the proposed M11 motorway at Bishops Stortford in Hertfordshire. The expert who was called in to deal with the problem was a member of a field sports organisation. It was reported that he would move in and dig the animals up when they are asleep. A spokesperson said: "They will go into the area with Jack Russell terriers, the dogs will go down the holes and pull the badgers out by their tails." The so-called expert was asked to deal with the badgers by the Eastern Road Construction Unit, on behalf of the Department of the Environment.

I later visited the claimed expert at his home in Nottinghamshire where he showed me a pair of badger tongs and described how he removed the badgers from their sett using tongs. He also showed me a badger skull which had a fractured jaw caused he said by grasping the badger by the jaw with the tongs when removing it. This he claimed was the best way to take the animal from its sett. The badgers when taken he said, were released into a new home in Nottinghamshire.

In a badger baiting session a shallow pit is dug ready to receive a badger when it has been taken from its sett. This pit is used to keep the animal from fleeing its tormentors during the baiting session, the dogs are egged on with shouts and yells to attack the unfortunate animal. Sometimes baiting pits are dug in remote locations such as disused farmyards, or as I have seen several times, in woodlands sometimes not far from an active sett.

I have in my possession a video of a badger baiting session lasting for some ninety minutes. This was handed in by the diggers themselves (presumably for cash) to the *Sunday People* newspaper who alerted the authorities resulting in a successful prosecution of those who took part in the baiting session. In the video sequence, a badger is put into a shallow pit and dogs of every conceivable type from terrier to bull mastiff are encouraged to attack the unfortunate badger that did not want to fight. The badger tucks its head under the chest and puts its forelegs over the head and only reacts with a brief snap at the dogs when it is bitten. Ultimately when the badger tires of its torture and tries to rest by refusing to respond to the bites, it is roused by its tormenters by having bricks thrown at it; this was to get it to stir so that the dogs can continue the savagery. When the badger is almost dead the baiters then stab the animal several times when it mercifully expires. Badgers are reluctant to fight, as evidenced by the video. During the video sequence the badger never initiates the attack and only responds when it is bitten itself.

Another incident concerning badger baiting occurred in Mansfield, Nottinghamshire when a chemist was asked to develop and print a film. On completing the processing the chemist was appalled at what he saw on the prints, they showed a badger being baited by two bull terrier type dogs. The dogs were grasping the badger, one each side of the animals face. The chemist printed a duplicate set of prints and walked onto the street outside the shop where a police officer was just passing by and was shown the prints. He immediately recognised the back yard and the greenhouse where the baiting had taken place. The police officer then followed up the incident and the offenders were successfully prosecuted for the cruelty offences. When asked in court what had subsequently happened to the unfortunate badger, the men claimed it was released back into the wild, I doubt very much that the magistrates or any one present in court believed this.

On Boxing Day 1981 I received a telephone call from a landowner at Flintham, a village in Nottinghamshire, who told me he had found a badger in suspicious circumstances close to a sett situated in a plantation on his land. I went to investigate and found a badger with a strong rope tied tightly around its neck with chafing wounds to the neck showing the animal had been trying to escape. With its mouth open and filled with soil, we concluded that the badger was taken from the sett and baited on the spot.

Poison gas was commonly used by gamekeepers to deal with foxes, although originally developed for use against rabbits and moles it was extensively used against carnivores, especially when it was suspected that a fox had taken refuge in a badger sett. One deadly substance was a poison called Cymag, mentioned earlier. The powder was fed into the entrances of rabbit warrens, or fox earths and sometimes badger setts, by a spoon tied to a stick. The entrances to the tunnels were then sealed by earth and the substance would then react to the dampness in the tunnels producing a deadly hydrocyanic gas. The animals, in particular badgers, would normally retreat from the gas underground and in the case of badgers could starve to death rather than enter the tunnels containing the gas.

In a Nottinghamshire parish there is a wood with a typical large badger sett. The wood was part of a large estate and a gamekeeper was employed to look after the reared game. A lady farmer lived in a farmhouse appropriately named Brockwood Farm, next to the wood. Whilst attending to the livestock one day, she looked towards the wood and noticed the gamekeeper leaving the wood near to the badger sett.

Being of a suspicious nature she decided to visit the wood and check the

Flora Johnson

sett. Arriving at the sett she noticed a strong smell of an acrid nature and noticed that all the entrances to the sett appeared to have been blocked with earth. Looking for a large stick she set about opening the main entrance. She saw a badger appearing to be either dead or unconscious. At some risk from the gas (later identified as Cymag) she dragged the badger with a foreleg away from the entrance and left it on the sett. Returning a little while later she saw the badger had recovered and was making its way underground.

The farmer contacted the landowner with the news of the incident, knowing of her interest in the badgers he was most helpful and contacted his keeper who gave some explanation and showed his employer what he claimed to be badger prints leading into the entrances of the sett.

How did I learn of the keeper's actions at the sett? Some years after he had retired I visited him at his home, by which time he had become a wealthy man having inherited through his wife's family a farm. During our friendly chat I brought up the question of setts gassed on the estate, and he freely admitted the gassing. He then told me of the incident where he went to the sett before showing the landowner, and laughing he described how he made imprints with his knuckles imitating the footprints of a badger leading into the entrances. The landowner was completely satisfied with his keeper's explanation. Happily though, the sett continues to be active to this day.

During the years before the badger protection legislation it was perfectly legal for men to visit a badger sett with dogs and to dig them out. Sometimes they were advertised for sale in local newspapers as pets. Examples of these are from advertisements In the *Nottingham Evening Post* one dated June 1968 "Badger cub for sale, Oxton, Nottinghamshire". Another advertisement in the same paper dated May 1972 read "Badger cubs for sale £6 each" and gave an address in Trowell, Nottinghamshire. I contacted this advertiser pretending an interest and was told that the cubs had been sold but they said that they could obtain one for me if I could wait until the weekend. I declined the offer after making a bogus excuse I broke off the conversation.

Other advertisements offered dogs for sale, one such read: "Terrier, will go down to fox and badger, can be seen working if required, South Normanton, Nottinghamshire." During the 1972 Newark Agricultural Show, badger pelts were being offered for sale. They were seen by a badger-friendly farmer, she informed the show secretary and then contacted me. The seller was believed to have come from Walsall, Birmingham. The show secretary later telephoned me to say that he was determined that badger pelts would not be sold at any future shows.

The campaign to protect the badger began in the late 1960s/early1970s when a number of organisations became active in trying to protect the animal. In particular the Women's Institute was very active in lobbying and raising the profile of the badger as numerous cases of baiting and other cruel practices were making the headlines. Other groups who had experience of badger digging and baiting were also making their voices heard. Among these groups were the Frodsham Badger Group and the Mammal Society's Badger Group.

Dr Ernest Neal who often chaired the Mammal Society Badger Group meetings was in touch with Lord Arran. The Earl had for some years kept a badger as a pet and was aware of the severe levels of persecution. He was eager to get some protection for the animal and was prepared to introduce a Private Members Bill in the House of Lords. Also concerned was Lord Cranbrook, then President of the Mammal Society, who assisted with the drafting of the Arran Bill.

Lord Cranbrook attended meetings of the Mammal Society's Badger Group where he made a contribution by suggesting various clauses to be drafted into the Bill. On one occasion the Earl sat beside me and we discussed various ways of strengthening the Bill. He told me he used to hunt and felt rather guilty, since hunting was a rich man's sport and badger digging was a poor man's sport. He confessed that he had not seen a live badger until he mentioned this to his daughter's boyfriend who promptly turned up the next morning with two badgers in a sack.

At the same meeting Lord Cranbrook spoke to me about badger tongs which up to then I had never seen, and asked if I would put it to the meeting that it become illegal to use badger tongs in the course of killing or taking, or attempting to kill or take, any badger.

This was put to the meeting and was accepted and appeared in the 1973 Badgers Act in Section 2 and was carried through to the 1992 Protection of Badgers Act.

Under the Arran Bill the sett itself was not specially protected except, for example, in a nature reserve. Around the same time the Arran Bill was introduced in the Lords, Peter Hardy, who was MP for Rother Valley (later Lord Hardy of Wath), introduced a private members Bill in the Commons. This was a less strong Bill than the Arran Bill.

Peter Hardy's Bill was in case the Arran Bill was opposed and fell. A certain amount of give and take became necessary because of the field sports lobby in the Lords and in the House of Commons. Fox hunting peers and MPs in the Commons were concerned that protecting badgers might interfere with, for example, the practice of blocking badger setts and earths and drains to prevent foxes going to ground during a fox hunt.

Before the Badger Bills mentioned reached the House of Commons for the various stages, Peter Hardy MP wrote to a number of individuals interested in conservation of the badger and its plight. He asked if I, along with Dr Ernest Neal and Dr Richard Paget, would like to attend as badger experts as part of a delegation to visit the Home Office, and talk to the

Minister for Home Affairs about persecution of badgers that was rife at that time. The delegation would also include himself and an opposition MP, David James, who represented North Dorset (both MPs had interests in badgers and I believe Mr James had badgers on his land).

We travelled to London on Monday 16th April 1973 and met MPs Peter Hardy and David James at the House of Commons and after watching a session of the Commons in action we visited the tea-rooms for refreshments. We later met up with Baroness Young who was at that time Leader of the House of Lords.

The delegation then continued with a short walk to the Home Office led by the Baroness. On the way we were discussing various problems and the Baroness praised Ernest's first book on the badger in the Collins Monograph Series, first published in 1948.

Arriving at the Home Office we were introduced to the Minister Lord Colville by Baroness Young. Ernest outlined the position regarding the plight of the badger, which included the baiting of badgers, digging out of the animals and of the unrelenting tormenting and interference with badgers in the name of so-called sport. I was able to give Ernest the situation in Nottinghamshire having typed out a sheet giving examples of snaring, digging and badger cubs being offered for sale in local papers. The Minister was sympathetic but said he had received much emotional correspondence but no first-hand evidence of persecution at his department. Richard and I offered to collect such evidence from the Mammal Society Badger Recorders and forward this to the Home Office and hopefully secure Government support for one of the Bills.

We wrote to all the Mammal Society Recorders asking for evidence of persecution and received much information including a reply from a senior official of an exclusive hunt telling of an annual Boxing Day dig for badgers where a Master of Hounds took part along with hunt employees, taking along a flagon of cider for refreshment. This activity was not illegal at the time but was frowned on by most country people. We were also lent some graphic pictures of badger baiting, showing a tethered badger being baited by seven dogs.

Jane Ratcliffe, author of *Through the Badger Gate*, had managed to obtain photographs of a badger baiting incident, where a former participant had become disgusted with the activity and had gone along on a dig and covertly taken pictures of the events. He dared not reveal the faces of the

Jane Ratcliff

diggers but still provided good evidence of the cruel practices. Jane was happy to lend the pictures to us and these were sent to the Home Office along with the other submissions. This information helped to secure support from within government for the proposed legislation. The Arran Bill became law in 1973 and its provisions were later incorporated into the Protection of Badgers Act of 1992 along with the Badgers Act 1991 and the Badgers (Further Protection) Act 1991 with much stronger protection for the sett as well as the animal, and penalties were also increased.

Renardine, a pungent bone oil substance commonly used against foxes as a deterrent, was at one time licensed for use against badgers, however, on March 24th 2005 this substance was banned for any use. There are now no chemical deterrents licensed for use against badgers.

In spite of many decades of persecution badgers continue to thrive and although there is a high rate of mortality in young animals reckoned at around 60%, some animals survive to reach what might be described as old age, in the wild this might be around seven to ten years, although in captivity this could be much longer. I have heard of a captive animal in

Yorkshire which lived as long as seventeen years.

I have in my possession a badger skull from Woodchester Park in Gloucestershire I estimate to be at least ten years old. This skull shows obvious signs of old age such as teeth so completely worn down that the animal was chewing on the jawbone, a number of the teeth were also completely missing. The photograph shows the extent of the wear and tear of the dentition probably causing the badger considerable pain before its demise. Richard Paget examined the skull and found that osteoarthritis, was caused by an infection entering through the cavity left by a missing canine tooth. Adrian Middleton also found that badgers suffer many similar signs of aging as is found in other mammals including humans. When conducting a post-mortem of an old badger found dead at a sett at Mirfield, West Yorkshire he found the animal had suffered from extensive arteriosclerosis (hardening of the arteries). This was confirmed on histological examination of the tissues by Dr Keith Bradbury, pathologist at the School of Medicine, Leeds.

The main cause of mortality in badgers is most likely the result of road casualties, up to 50,000 badgers are estimated to be killed in this way each year.

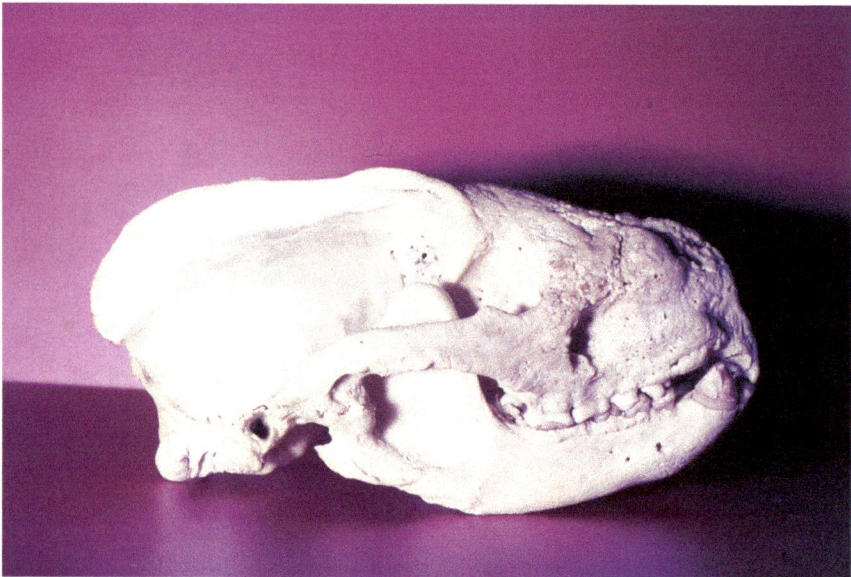

Fox Earth or Badger Sett?

Many years ago I decided to construct an artificial fox earth hopefully with a chance of photographing foxes and their cubs. With this in mind I enlisted the help of a friend, Peter Shakespeare, and my son Stephen to build an artificial fox earth. Not having enough room to excavate underground chambers we decided to make the earth above ground.

A friend who was working with a large engineering company managed to get some lined metal pipes, 30cm in diameter, to make the tunnel entrances. There would be one entrance in the garden and a second one leading into the permanent pasture at the back of the house. We decided to make a single chamber with brick-built sides measuring around a metre in length and 65cm in width with a concrete slab for the roof. The walls of the earth were double sided and in-filled with brick rubble. This was to provide a *hibernacula* for newts and other *amphibia.*

The earth when completed was covered with soil to provide some warmth and a bed for wild flowers. Although foxes have never bred in the earth they have used it on occasions. In particular dog foxes during the mating season have often stayed in the earth for a few days. Also several foxes have lived in it when injured. In particular one dog fox seemed to sustain injuries to its hind legs on a regular basis and stay in the earth for several days until the wounds had healed.

On one occasion a fox was seen in the garden when an aircraft flew very low over the garden making a loud noise shaking the house and the surrounding area. I saw the fox dart into the earth as the aircraft passed overhead where it stayed for around twenty minutes. The next day the press reported an aeroplane heading for East Midlands Airport had made a safe landing when one of the engines had failed. This was the explanation for the noise and the fox's dash for the earth.

Although the foxes only used the earth sporadically, an animal that stayed there for four months was a badger. On the evening of the 8th of October 2009 I was looking out of the window when the security light came on at 7.30pm. I was astonished to see a fully-grown sow badger in the garden. After rooting around for a while it went into the earth and stayed there for a while and then re-appeared through the hedge. It must have emerged from the field entrance and made its way back into the garden. After a while the badger went back into the earth. The animal spent sometime there and when next seen was peeping out of the entrance.

I stayed up late that night and was rewarded with seeing the badger feeding on earthworms around the edges of the lawn where it seemed the worms congregated. I was able to watch the badger taking worms right under the dining room window at a range of around two metres and could clearly see the technique where the animal would run forward and seize the worm near the head and with a jerk pull the worm out and gobble it up. Having taken all the available worms on the back lawn the badger then moved to the front garden where it carried out the same procedure working the edges of the lawns and then moving to the middle of the lawn and working the grass edging around the pond.

Once the badger had settled in for a few days it marked the earth by making a large dung pit above the entrance leading into the garden. A few days later I checked the garden for other signs, sure enough there were dung pits in each corner of the garden, the badger was marking its territory very precisely. One surprising observation was the amount of drinking the animal did. Usually within a short time of emergence the badger would visit the wild pond in the back garden and quench its thirst.

I took advantage of this behaviour pattern by setting up a camera and flash and taking a picture. The badger always drank at the same place each night so was predictable. Other types of behaviour after emergence were observed and would consist of scratching and grooming and scent marking.

To take some photographs I placed a few peanuts in the middle of the lawn. The badger soon found these and on a few nights was seen eating together with a fox, although the fox always gave way when the badger moved towards it. If the fox arrived before the badger had emerged it would go to the earth and sniff at the entrance presumably to see if there was anyone at home.

Occasionally the badger could be seen peeping out of the earth quite early around 5pm in October before emerging around 9pm. On mild nights we would see the badger come into the garden through a gap in the thorn hedge and we assumed it had been worming in the pasture at the back of the garden and had emerged from the field entrance.

On very windy nights the badger would emerge much later. I have noticed this when watching at a number of setts and have assumed that this is because the animals have difficulty in distinguishing between friendly and possibly unfriendly sounds, and are therefore much more cautious before emerging. Once they leave the sett on such nights they seem to leave without any of the usual grooming sessions and make off into the night fairly quickly.

December was a very cold month with snow falling and the ponds frozen. On the 18th of the month the badger was seen walking across the ice on the back pond that had received a light fall of snow. The next morning I was able to take photographs of the badger's prints where it had walked the perimeter of the frozen pond. Whilst watching the badger a few nights later

I was delighted to see a barn owl fly across the garden just above the badger's head. What an amazing picture that would have made, quite impossible to anticipate of course!

During the severe weather we bought small bales of hay for the badger to take in for bedding. The hay was left on the lawn and was soon taken into the earth, or perhaps it should now be called a sett. Although the fox would always sniff in the artificial earth when he came to visit he not surprisingly made no attempt to enter. He would of course know immediately of the badger's presence and would not attempt to enter whilst it was occupied.

Not sleeping well one night on the 5th January 2010, I looked out of the window at 3.20am and saw the badger taking in the hay for bedding. The animal must have worked hard that night because by daylight a large pile of hay had been taken into the earth with only a few wisps remaining.

On the night of the 6th of January there was a heavy fall of snow blocking one of the roads from the village and the badger stayed in the earth for a few nights. It was next seen on the 8th of January leaving the earth, after that it was not observed until the 26th of January at 7.45pm, when it stayed near the entrance of the earth for a mammoth grooming session. The last time it was seen was the 31st January. The badger I believe was a sow about to produce cubs when she perhaps realised that the small earth was not suitable to house a family and moved out. The

pipe mentioned under artificial setts was I believe her next refuge. The pipe was situated about 250 metres away from the house and being some eighty metres long offered much more space than our small earth. The pipe showed signs of more recent activity with bedding and a polished surface near the entrance.

We enjoyed the badger's stay with us and certainly learned something seeing the animal behaving naturally in close up, and for the opportunity to see the relationship between badger and fox on a nightly basis. We weren't sorry when it moved on as our neighbours were being visited and some snuffle holes on their immaculate lawn were not exactly to be welcomed.

Dr Ernest G. Neal (The Badger Man)

Ernest Neal is mentioned here because of the enormous contribution he has made to our knowledge of the *Eurasian* badger not only through his writings on the animal from his first book *The Badger,* published in 1948, and his last book with Chris Cheesman, *Badgers,* published in 1996. He was mainly responsible for the huge interest in the badger now shown by the many groups and individuals keen to foster an interest in the animal and its protection.

Ernest, as he was known to his friends, chaired many meetings of the then Mammal Society Badger Group with great firmness refusing any politicising of a subject under discussion; he always remained neutral and polite even with those he disagreed with. His autobiography, *The Badger Man,* mentions the visit we made to the Home Office in support of the draft Bills aiming protection for badgers then being presented to Parliament.

We wrote regularly to each other, Ernest was always helpful with advice and I was pleased to assist when he asked for help with a badger problem near Doncaster in Yorkshire. Ernest was at this time rather elderly and unable to visit the site personally. Two lady farmers who were wildlife enthusiasts had a colony of badgers threatened when a public path was proposed. The pathway would have crossed over the sett and the immediate foraging area. Ernest asked if I could visit the farm and assess the problem and offer advice. I visited the farm and saw the sett in question in October 1996 and wrote a report on the situation, offering advice to the council officer responsible who agreed to ask the council to divert the proposed footpath. This was done and the farmers were delighted, thanking us profusely. This was typical of Ernest who at this time was elderly and frail yet still wanted to help with the situation and in particular the badgers who were threatened with huge disturbance.

I last met with Ernest and his wife Betty in January 1998 when he invited myself and my wife to visit him where he lived in Bedfordshire; we spent the day discussing badgers and other wildlife and looked at the many photographs of badgers and some he had taken in Africa including a fine picture of dancing cranes, which hung in his study. We went for lunch and when we returned we carried on our talks on wildlife matters, Ernest's little Jack Russell dog Tara sitting on his knee no doubt missing his daily walk with his master in the park opposite the house. Sadly a few weeks after our visit, Ernest passed away. His funeral on the 28th of April 1998 was attended by many of his friends from the fields of science, education and conservation. Ernest Neal is gone but we well remember him for his delightful writings on the badger and his vast knowledge of many other species.

Stoats, Weasels and other *Mustelids*

Stoats (*Mustela erminea*) and weasels (*Mustela nivalis*) are some of the most difficult animals to observe in the wild. Being carnivores they spend time hunting by day and night in short forays. When not hunting much time is spent sleeping, often in rabbit holes, or drainage pipes when dry, they have also been found using badger setts as resting places. These lying up places are found scattered throughout the territory. On a private estate a friend has built an artificial stoat or weasel den using drainage pipes as entrances and a mound of large boulders covering small chambers. The whole thing is topped with a plastic liner for waterproofing and covered with a layer of smaller boulders and stones. The den is situated in a dry ditch. On a recent visit we were delighted to see a weasel using the den, emerging and running around the area.

Behaviour

The stoat, unlike the weasel, produces only one litter a year after a period of delayed implantation as in its larger cousin the badger, whereas the weasel can produce up to two litters a year with no delayed implantation. The stoats mate in the summer and the young are born the following spring in March or April. The weasels breeding season lasts from early spring into the summer.

Stoats mainly take larger prey such as rabbits and rats as well as some smaller animals such as wood mice and voles. Small birds may be taken as nestlings or stalked as adults. A friend once observed a stoat jump and catch a green woodpecker that was resting on a small tree stump. Although a rare occurrence and unfortunate for the woodpecker it shows the incredible agility of the stoat.

Not all the rabbits chased are successfully taken as prey, since on occasion the rabbits do fight back. I well remember one such occasion whilst walking in Bradgate Park in Leicestershire. There is a well-established rabbit warren next to the reservoir in the park and when I was walking close to the warren I became aware of a young rabbit being pursued by a stoat. The rabbit was running in ever decreasing circles with the stoat close on its tail. When it was close enough the stoat leapt upon the back of the rabbit, whereupon the rabbit squealed and immediately three adult rabbits appeared from the undergrowth and using their hind legs kicked off the stoat from the rabbit's back. This all happened in the space of a few seconds. I later searched the area where the action had taken place but could find no trace of rabbits or stoat and could only assume that the young rabbit had escaped with its life and the stoat had wisely departed.

Some stoats in the northern limits of their range turn white in the winter months. In Scotland they are regularly seen as white except for the black tip to their tails. Reports of stoats in ermine have been made from more lowland areas but these observations are much less common than those in the northern regions. There was a reliable report of a white stoat in south Nottinghamshire during a severe winter in January 1987, when the Curator of Biology at Nottingham Natural History Museum, Wollaton Hall, Dr Sheila Wright, was riding a horse through woodland when she saw a stoat in ermine. Sheila recorded her sighting and let me know of her observation.

The fur of the stoat when in ermine was used for the trimmings on the cloaks of judges and peers as seen in the annual parade of judges and peers proceeding to the House of Lords for the State Opening of Parliament. I often wonder how many stoats have been sacrificed to dress their lordships in their finery.

Our smallest carnivore the weasel concentrates on the smaller prey items such as mice and voles but will also take young rabbits and rats and sometimes amphibians. I once observed a weasel in the springtime near a pond where dozens of spawning toads were splashing and croaking in the water, many were male toads unpaired. The weasel ran along a log towards the noisy melee of toads and jumped into the water seizing a toad behind the head and ran back along the log carrying its prey. When it was near the end of the log it dived into the long grass, appearing a little while later minus the toad.

This pattern of catching was repeated around a dozen times, with toads as the prey items although once a single frog was caught. Each time the pattern was the same, the toad being disabled by a bite to the back of the head and carried to what I assume was a den, perhaps housing young. I was concerned what effect this predation would have on the frog and toad population but on reflection all the toads caught were males. Since the majority of toads were in *amplexus* and thus spawning, it seems the weasel was taking the surplus males. The single bite to the back of the head would paralyse the frog or toad and it would remain fresh until required.

Whilst entertaining friends and relatives one Boxing Day we were treated to some amusing antics when a weasel came into the garden and

climbed on top of the artificial fox earth and scampered through the earth and reappeared from the other side of the hedge and searched through our log pile. The weasel spent about fifteen minutes in and around the garden before leaving. The following day friends at the other end of the village reported seeing a weasel running along the hedgerow, we assumed it was the weasel who had provided us with entertainment the previous day.

Both stoats and weasels can be called up by sucking on the back of the hand and making a squeaking noise. This technique is useful for attracting the animals to get a better view or take a photograph. I have managed to get pictures of stoats using this method, finding it works better on stoats than weasels.

Whilst holidaying in Scotland I was watching a stoat running along a ditch towards me so I ran to the car to pick up a camera only to see the stoat disappear into a pile of boulders. I decided to try to call it up by making a squeaking sound by sucking on the back of the hand, sure enough it appeared from a gap in the pile of boulders and I was able to get a photograph. I tried the same technique several more times, but was disappointed as further callings were totally ignored. Gamekeepers and those involved in game shooting are aware of these techniques and their efforts usually result in a blast of lead shot rather than a photograph.

Once whilst watching badgers I was approached several times by a weasel wanting to pass exactly where I was standing. The animal approached right up to my feet and standing on its hind legs looked up at me before retreating. This took place several times before I decided to move to one side allowing the animal to continue to its destination without me obstructing it.

Both stoats and weasels are curious animals and investigate pipes and other man-made contraptions, sadly these are often laid out to attract the animals on game shooting estates and often house Fenn traps. These traps are spring-loaded and snap round the body of the animal when it enters the pipe.

The life span of both stoats and weasels is determined by the availability of food, particularly in the winter months when prey species are in reduced numbers, or are more difficult to catch when the ground cover is reduced by the wintry conditions. In these conditions prey have a better chance of seeing the approach of a predator and are able to take evasive action.

The number of weasels getting through winter is around 25% of the population, a proportion of those animals making it through to spring could possibly survive into a third year. In captivity most animals could survive for several years longer than in the wild, where they are protected from food shortages and predation and housed in favourable conditions.

In my young days I once kept a weasel as a pet for a while until my mother decided it was time for the animal to be released back into the wild. Whilst I was wandering through the graveyard of a country church I heard a weak mewing sound and upon looking down was surprised to see a tiny weasel on top of a coltsfoot leaf. I picked up the animal and put it in my jacket pocket where it soon settled down, no doubt enjoying the warmth of the pocket, and transported it home by bicycle. On arriving home I fed and watered the weasel and it soon settled down and was scuttling round the living room before being housed in a small cage. Every evening the weasel would be allowed to investigate its surroundings before being enticed into the cage and kept in for the night. The right thing was decided when, as explained, it was released back into the wild. The interesting thing about the weasel is that it never attempted to bite whilst kept as a pet.

In Ireland there are no weasels and the Irish stoat is usually smaller than its mainland cousin although they are really the same animal. The Irish stoat has an irregular line marking the division between the white belly fur and the brown fur on the upper body. The stoats in mainland Britain have a straight bodyline dividing the white fur of the underbelly from the brown fur of the upper body. Stoats in mainland Britain are not protected, whilst those in the Irish Republic are protected by law.

The Polecat (*Mustela putorius*)

The polecat is smaller than a pine marten but bigger than a stoat and in the past few decades has greatly increased its range by spreading from its stronghold in Wales. Like all *mustelids* the polecat has anal scent glands which emit a foul smelling scent which is capable of deterring a predator and assists in territorial marking. Because of the foul smell the polecat makes when disturbed or alarmed it is sometimes known as a foulmart or foul marten. In my home county of Nottinghamshire several road casualty polecats have been checked by me, these have proved to be genuine polecats rather than polecat-ferret crosses. There are also reliable reports of polecats being caught in Fenn traps in south Nottinghamshire.

Polecats are capable of breeding with ferrets, ferreters have been known to cross a ferret with a polecat, hence polecat-ferrets. I have in my possession several skulls of ferrets or polecat-ferrets thrown out of badger setts when the occupants have been cleaning out the sett. These were presumably the remains of animals lost during rabbiting sessions and were either killed by the badgers or perished in some other way underground.

There is no delayed implantation with polecats, after mating the young are produced after a gestation period lasting forty-two days, eyelids and ears are closed and the young become independent of their parents when they are aged between two to three months old.

My own sightings of live polecats are confined to the Snowdonia area of Wales.

Once taking the footpath near Nantgwynant to Mount Snowdon I became aware of a rabbit warren in a hedgerow on the left of the footpath. To my amazement a polecat came out of one of the entrances to the warren, on seeing us it disappeared into the warren only to reappear from another entrance further along the footpath. I tried to squeak it out again but it would not resurface. We once stayed at a cottage in the area where the owner, a schoolmaster, told us that during the winter he had a polecat lying up in his garage for several weeks.

The food of polecats consists of any animal from hares to smaller mammals such as mice and voles, they will also eat amphibians and reptiles as well as insects. They are said to cache live amphibians such as frogs and toads after disabling them by a bite to the base of the skull and storing them in a paralysed state until required. A similar behaviour pattern has been described with the weasel earlier.

Pine Marten (*Martes martes*)

The pine marten is probably the most attractive of the smaller *mustelids* with its lovely reddish brown coat and creamy white on the throat. In size it is larger than the polecat with a large bushy tail. Like the stoat there is a period of delayed implantation after mating which usually takes place in midsummer; after implantation the young are born in the following spring in March/April. The young are born blind and deaf and are able to leave the den when around ten weeks old, although staying close by for another few weeks following their mother around.

Pine martens use a variety of dens or lying up places that may be a hollow tree or tree hole, they also utilise crevices among rock piles and artificial places such as large nest boxes put up for owls. In some cases martens have been known to occupy loft spaces or outbuildings. Being excellent climbers the animals are sometimes seen in the trees during the daytime although they are mainly nocturnal and are frequently seen crossing the roads at night

The stronghold of the pine marten in Britain is in the Highlands of Scotland and in Ireland, although there are small populations in North Wales and in the Lake District and it is said that they are present in Yorkshire.

Feeding consists of birds and small rodents, as well as beetles and grubs. Vegetable matter is also eaten especially berries and fruits in the autumn. Martens living near human habitations are often fed with bread thickly spread with jam, apparently raspberry jam is a favourite.

Whilst holidaying on the Ardnamurchan Peninsula in western Scotland some years ago I asked the locals about pine martens. For good reasons some people were rather loth to reveal the areas which martens were known to frequent. Although fairly widespread in the area, local knowledge can save much time searching for animals. Once I had made contact with a local naturalist and he was assured of my interest, I was told of a farmer who was feeding pine martens every evening.

The next day I visited the farmer and asked if we could watch the pine martens when he was feeding them. We were then invited to visit the farm that evening and offered tea whilst we waited for the pine martens visit. Shortly after dark, slices of bread were laced with raspberry jam and placed on the window ledge, jam was also spread on the newly furbished window frames. We then sat back and waited for the entertainment to start.

Eventually the martens turned up and the windows were opened and a beautiful female marten came through the window and was followed by two youngsters, they all set about eating the sandwiches and licking the jam from the sill. The show lasted for about half an hour and then the animals returned to the wooded area just outside. During the visit of the martens I managed to take a few flash photographs and was able to send some pictures to the friendly farmer who was pleased to have pictures of the martens in his kitchen.

Visiting the area the next day in the daytime we were able to detect the presence of the pine martens by finding their droppings in the woods, and evidence of their rootings in the leaf litter. We also found droppings along the roadside. The faeces we found were rather sticky mucilaginous deposits showing the remains of fruits and berries, although we also found some which showed the remains of small mammals, presumably rodents such

as voles and wood mice, others we found contained fragments of feathers. Some locals told us that they thought the pine martens were having an impact on the small bird population, however, we found large numbers of small birds in the area especially chaffinches which seemed to be the commonest birds around.

Friends who have been holidaying in Scotland in the past few years have managed to take some excellent photographs of martens at a baiting site near their chalet. They also managed to get a badger and a marten in the same picture feeding together.

Once whilst holidaying in North Wales we were told that our host had seen two martens crossing the rough area in front of the house we were staying in. This was reliable information as other people in the area spoke of the presence of the pine marten. Although occurring in smaller numbers in Wales than further north, martens are able to take advantage of the extensive coniferous plantations now found in North Wales and hopefully will become more common in future years.

Adrian Middleton

The Otter (*Lutra lutra*)

The otter is a favourite animal with those who have an interest in wildlife. They are a member of the *mustelid* family and next in size to the badger, the largest member of the family.

Breeding

In the otter there is no delayed implantation and the young are born some 62/63 days after mating. Most cubs are born during late spring and the summer months, usually between May and August. The average litter size is two to three cubs, the number of cubs may vary because of the quality of feeding in particular areas. The better the food supply the more likely for a bitch otter to produce more than a single cub. The young will stay with their mother for up to a year.

Territorial marking is usually carried out by leaving droppings known as spraints on prominent features such as rocks on the seashore or on the footings of bridges and other raised areas. In the case of rock markings, particularly those on sea lochs in northern areas, a form of algae grows from the spraints forming a green colouring which seems to be brighter and lighter as the algae ages. Thus by walking the seashore one can soon learn to spot the spraint markings by looking for the green colouring on the stones.

Feeding

Feeding is varied but mainly dictated by what is available at a particular area and the time of the year. In Scotland I have watched otters feeding in the sea lochs on the Ardnamurchan Peninsula. The animals were catching a variety of sea creatures such as lumpsuckers and sea urchins, smaller fish were eaten in the water. Larger prey items such as the sea urchins were brought out on to dry land to be consumed. In the case of otters living near coastal areas prey items are brought on to the lochside or seashore. Hooded crows were always ready to eat up the remains after the otters had finished. Often when otters are feeding in a sea loch the hooded crows can be seen waiting on the shore for the otters to come ashore with their quarry.

Otters in Scotland can be seen feeding at any time of the day but early morning is usually a good time for a sighting. Once whilst waiting for a glimpse of an otter early one misty morning I was rewarded by the sight of a dog otter which came within two metres of where I was standing. It then sprainted on an outflow pipe and disappeared into the mist. I was able to photograph the otter but the result was simply a silhouette of the animal because of the misty conditions.

In the rest of Britain otters are usually nocturnal, although there are many examples of daytime sightings, and in some cases the animals seem to become habituated to humans and are regularly seen during the daytime hours. Recently a friend who was checking for bats at night along the River Soar in Leicestershire saw an otter close by, and by using his torch was able to follow the otter as it crossed the river and lolloped away along the opposite bank.

Shortly after the reported sighting on the River Soar, I was collecting bird seed from my supplier, and whilst he was loading the seed into my car I asked him if he had been fishing lately. He then told me of an early morning fishing trip at Holme Pierrepont in south Nottinghamshire when he had good sightings of an otter fishing on the River Trent.

This reminded me of a fishing trip to North Wales when I was around fourteen years of age. Along with some friends we set up camp alongside the River Glaslyn that feeds Lake Gwynant. We fished the lake that was very shallow until after dark and soon caught enough small brown trout for breakfast.

We piled a collection of trout on the bank ready for morning and then waded out into the lake and carried on fishing. The banks of the river were quite high and on the far bank we could see what appeared to be large animals running along the bankside above our heads. One of our party

became quite worried and thought there were dogs loose nearby, however, it soon became apparent that these were a family of otters and after a while we could hear them whistling their contact calls.

Whilst we were seeing the otters we could hear the baying of otter hounds (hunting was still legal at the time) appearing to come from up the valley. When we had finished fishing we went to collect our catch to prepare them for breakfast. To our amazement every fish had its shoulder eaten away. We then realised that the otters had helped themselves to our catch, eating the best parts of each fish, this meant that we would have to rise early to replenish our breakfast. I for one didn't begrudge the otters their treat as the trout were small and easy to catch and these were the first otters I had ever seen.

The member of our fishing expedition who was originally scared of the otters thinking they might be dogs told me of a way he used to get trout by waiting for an otter to catch a trout.

This took place on the River Greet near Southwell in Nottinghamshire. He would wait on a bridge and when an otter caught a trout and brought it ashore to eat he would clap his hands and scare the otter away then retrieve the fish for himself. Rather unfair for the otter but he claimed that both otters and brown trout were common then, this being in the 1950s.

My next experience of otters was when some four years after the Welsh sightings I was fishing in County Clare in the Irish Republic. I had asked a landowner if I could fish on his stretch of the river. Permission was granted

without charge and the owner showed me his stretch of the river. We stood above a weir chatting and looking for the best place to fish. Whilst we were talking an otter swam round the pool below us and then disappeared, this was around midday and we had a perfect sighting of the animal.

I fished the river and whilst wandering along the bank I lost my landing net, when leaving for my lodgings I called on the landowner and told him of my misfortune and he promised to look for the lost net. Visiting the area a few days later I called for news of the landing net and was told he had found the net and it was passed on to me. I tried to reward him for his patience and perseverance (he had spent three days searching for the net) but he refused to accept any reward. We chatted about the otters and I asked him if he ever saw badgers at night. He said that he did and told me he hated them, and when he saw them at night he would shoot them. Apparently he believed they were some kind of evil omen. It seemed strange that a man who clearly loved otters should hate one of its close relatives.

The next sighting of an otter was in 1973, the year of the first Badger Act. I had spent the day at the Attenborough Nature Reserve managed by the Nottinghamshire Wildlife Trust. I was looking for water voles that were at that time common on the reserve. I had seen a good number of voles during the day and as it was becoming dark I was crossing a bridge

heading for my car when I became aware of a movement in the water. At first I thought a water vole was foolishly swimming a long way from the shore and was in danger of a pike taking it. However, what I was seeing was the head of an otter looking about the size of a water vole. The animal then made for an island when I had good views as it lolloped along the bank, showing that it was an otter. Sadly the water voles seem to have disappeared from the area, however, otters are known to visit the reserve and may well breed there.

When not out feeding, or in the case of young animals playing, otters will make a nest in a reed bed and lie up there, cubs are known to have been born in such nests. Sometimes otters will dig under tree roots and make a holt, a more permanent lying up place than a nest in a reed bed. In Shetland, otters are known to excavate holts (a den or lying-up refuge) in the soft peaty soil usually close to the seashore and consisting of a number of entrances. Bedding is taken into the holt, the otter shuffling backwards with the material tucked under the chin or body rather like the badger (Kruuk 1995). Near the holt, otters will mark the area with droppings known as spraints, these act as a territorial indicator, warning other otter families or individuals that the holt is occupied. The faeces contain scent from the anal glands.

Holts are not permanently occupied like main badger setts but are used for breeding or as lying-up places between feeding areas. In the case of dog otters, these lying-up holts are used when patrolling the territory, which may consist of several miles of a river bank.

Many bodies such as the Wildlife Trusts are installing artificial otter holts along river banks and other suitable places thus helping with the otters to continue their recovery.

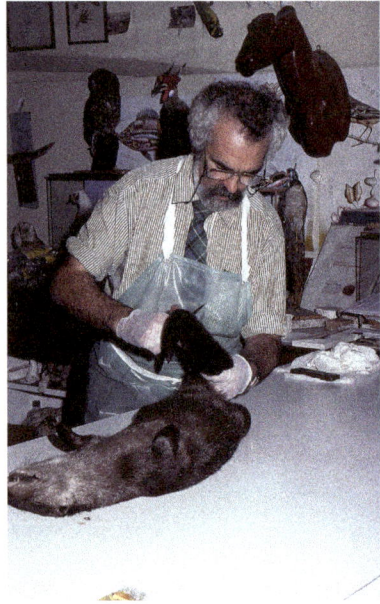

Don Sharp dissecting an Otter

Mink (*Mustela vison*)

The introduced American mink is another member of the weasel family or *mustelidae* which is now widespread and can be found over most of the British Isles and Ireland. They were imported for fur production in the late 1920s. Many animals either escaped from fur farms or were released presumably when the fur became unpopular and the cost of housing and feeding the animals became prohibitive.

Mink like some of the other *Mustelids* have a delayed implantation mechanism, meaning most young are born around twenty-eight days after implantation takes place. The number of young born varies but is usually around four to six, with most young being born in May.

The varied diet of the mink as a predator consists of animals as large as a rabbit to small rodents such as mice and voles. Ducks, coot and domestic fowls are eaten as well as fish of many species. Mink will take anything available and water voles where common are taken. In some areas mink have been known to locally exterminate water voles or cause them to move away from the area. The recent increase and spread of the otter is said to push mink from some areas, the otter being larger and dominant to mink. We now have otters on every river in Britain so it will be interesting to see what the long-term prospect is for the mink. Rather like the grey squirrel it seems the mink is here to stay.

A friend who worked for a large estate in south Nottinghamshire saw a mink come up from a lake on the estate and explore around the buildings around a quarter of a mile from the lake where the mink were occasionally seen. A large hollow tree on the edge of the lake was a cache where the mink stored fish in some quantity. The fish species stored in the bottom of the hollow tree consisted of roach, perch and carp.

My own experience of mink was when a local farmer asked for my opinion as to the predator when he was losing chickens on a nightly basis. He thought it was foxes but when I looked at the chicken pens, the chickens were being pulled downwards from under the raised coops through the wire mesh, not an easy task for a fox. We set some cage traps and baited them with chicken heads.

Visiting the traps the next morning we had caught a rather beautiful male mink, the animal was a very dark almost black with a shiny coat. Contrary to information I had heard from a mink hunter the mink was cowering in the trap and clearly terrified. I took pictures of the animal and then a decision had to be made as to its destruction. The farmer wanted to drown the mink in the trap but I was not happy with this method and took the mink to my local vet who euthanised it. The animal was then taken to the Wollaton Natural History Museum in Nottingham where the taxidermist was able to prepare it for display.

The Red Fox (*Vulpes vulpes*)

The red fox is our only member of the dog family (*Canidae*) in Britain and probably the most iconic animal of the British countryside. Loved or hated, the fox is one of the most successful carnivores in Britain and in spite of centuries of persecution by hunting, shooting, poisoning, snaring, or being dug out of its lair in the breeding season, it is still one of the most widespread animals throughout its range.

Red foxes are found throughout Europe and into Asia, different species of fox are found in the southern regions such as the small bat-eared fox and in the more northerly regions the arctic fox, which changes its coat to white during the severe winter months. This makes it one of the few carnivores along with the stoat to undergo a coat colour change to adapt to changing climatic conditions.

The success of the red fox is due to its varied diet and adaptability to changing conditions enabling the animal to exploit its environment. The increasing acceptance of foxes is also partly due to a more informed opinion in latter years, and the vast amount of factual information on the animal brought about by the many scientists who have studied foxes, notably Professors Stephen Harris and David McDonald, along with H. G. Lloyd, author of *The Red Fox,* and the many naturalists who see the animal on a daily basis and are able to correct the many false impressions of the fox.

Feeding

Foxes, although largely carnivorous, are perhaps more omnivorous than most people realise. Voles, especially short – tailed voles, are taken in numbers when available as well as wood mice and larger prey such as rabbits and hares. Although I have never seen a fox catch a hare I have seen the remains of hares near earths with a family of cubs present. I did, however, once see a hare following a fox. The fox was trying to catch voles by listening and then making the classic fox leap into the clumps of grass. The hare was a few metres behind the fox and every time the fox stopped to attempt to catch a vole, the hare waited until the fox either caught a vole, which it did several times, or failed, which happened more often. This trailing of the fox by the hare went on for the whole length of the field that was then down to set-aside, and consequently had tussocks of grass providing cover for small rodents such as voles and mice. Eventually the fox became aware of me and moved off, and the hare then gave up the game and lay down. The fox was well aware of the hare throughout, but probably knew it would be a waste of energy to try to pursue it because of the hare's superior turn of speed.

I have many times seen foxes catch rabbits either by waiting near warrens for the rabbits to emerge and then executing a quick burst of speed or, more usually, take the rabbits by stealth. This type of hunting entailed the fox sitting concealed in a hedgerow and, then waiting for a rabbit to run by or more usually waiting for a pair of rabbits to be chasing one another down a hedge-side and, with a quick dash from the hedge, taking the first rabbit and carrying it off to the waiting cubs. This way of taking prey I often witnessed from our house as it overlooks some permanent pasture which usually has a few rabbits present.

When the fox is not hunting, rabbits seem to be aware that they are not in any danger and will not panic or run away. I well remember seeing a group of rabbits feeding on the edge of a wood when a fox came out of the wood and went towards the rabbits.

The rabbits simply parted and the fox passed through them and then wandered off. The fox was not hunting and the rabbits were aware of this; when the fox had wandered off the rabbits came together again and resumed their feeding.

Rats are taken in some numbers and we especially welcome the foxes who take care of the rats visiting our garden during harvest time, when rats which have been living in the corn fields move from the disturbance and seek fresh cover nearer the village. At one of my study areas on a large arable farm surrounded by woodland, rats became a problem and a pest company was employed to put out poison traps round the farm buildings where the rats were taking stored grain. At that time there was a shooting syndicate who removed the foxes and other predators in order to protect the game birds as pheasants were reared in some numbers. Once the shooting was discontinued and a change in policy meant that the predators were no longer being removed the rat population reduced and eventually became scarce and the poison traps became redundant. The foxes are keeping the rats under control and are removing the rodents as they move in.

A friend once saw a fox which had caught a grey squirrel eat half of the animal and then continued to bury the remainder under a dried cow pat; a beekeeper friend also saw a fox catch a grey squirrel that was feeding on peanuts at one of my bird-feeding stations. When the fox suddenly appeared the squirrel dropped to the ground and made a dash for a tree but was beaten to it by the fox who grabbed the squirrel and made off with it into the undergrowth.

Carrion as road traffic kills, such as hedgehogs, rabbits and other animals, are taken. I have on many occasions seen foxes removing carcasses from the roads when driving after dark. Sometimes when the fox sees the approaching headlights they will retreat into the hedges and when the vehicle has passed will pop out and retrieve the carcass. Without the foxes as well as the crows, rooks and magpies cleaning up the carnage on a daily basis our roads would be littered with dead animals and other edible detritus left by ourselves.

Whilst out looking for foxes one morning I saw one coming from the direction of a farm carrying a chicken, it ate part of the chicken and then appeared to squat over the remains. I later checked the chicken carcass and found the fox had produced a scat (dropping) on top of the carcass. When hiding surplus food, the fox uses its nose to cover over the food usually seeking a natural hollow in the ground to save digging.

Foxes can and do take easily available domestic animals where these are not properly housed and are well able to take advantage of free range poultry if these are not shut away properly at night as I know to my cost. I used to keep a small flock of Light Sussex bantam chickens, which were shut away every evening. For some ten years we never lost a chicken to the foxes except for one evening when I left the door to the pen open; on checking the chickens the next morning I was met with the sight of an empty coop and all the chickens taken except for the odd carcass lying in the pen.

Amazingly some two weeks after the chickens had been taken, I was in the garden when I heard a clucking sound and my cockerel presumably must have scattered when the incident happened, suddenly appeared back home. Where he had been for some two weeks I have no idea, we live in open country so he must have survived by feeding on wild seeds and berries. How did he know where his home was? He had been born and bred within the confines of our small country garden.

I did not blame the foxes for taking the chickens, as I had been foolish enough to leave the door to the pen open giving our only member of the dog family a chance to get an easy meal. It is this opportunistic streak of the fox that enables it to survive and thrive in a countryside where game birds are reared in tens of millions. Inevitably a number of these non-indigenous birds are taken when winged (wounded but not killed), or are not able to take flight, or when they are unable to get off the ground properly because they are injured or their wings are not fully developed.

Urban foxes visit gardens on nightly forages where they can make a living feeding on earthworms and rodents such as rats and mice as well as handouts from those who enjoy seeing them.

When the ambient temperature is around 10 degrees centigrade and the earth is moist, earthworms appear on the surface of closely cropped pastures and mown garden lawns. They are taken in large numbers at night, and appear to be taken both by hearing and sight and perhaps by scent. Whilst worming on damp mild nights foxes seem to forage by listening for the worms moving by pricking the ears forward and tilting the head from side to side and then when very close moving forward and with a tug drawing the worm from its hole. Earthworms seem to keep the tail part of their body within the hole, presumably to make a quick retreat when threatened.

Insects such as beetles and flies are taken in quantity when available. I well remember being out in Derbyshire with a friend Irene Brierton using image Itensifier. We were observing both badgers and foxes. We were in a large pasture field where there was a tremendous emergence of crane flies (*Tipulids*) hatching from the ground. At one end of the field there was a family of foxes eating the flies and at the far end there was a badger family also taking advantage of this bonanza.

The animals were simply moving around the pasture randomly and picking up the emerging crane flies as they surfaced. Although the flies might seem rather small items for carnivores to take, they were able to eat dozens of the insects in a short time. By the end of the night they would have eaten their fill of this natural explosion of invertebrate food. We then moved onto a neighbouring pasture and with the help of our night-sights we were able to observe a fox carrying a small prey item, probably a short-tailed vole. Suddenly the fox veered away from us and started to chase a rabbit we had not noticed, both fox and rabbit disappeared over a hill so we were not able to see the end of the chase.

Foxes eat all kinds of fruits from blackberries, damsons and apples. When fed them they love grapes and other sweet fruits. Depending on the variety, apples are eaten but preference is for the soft fruits. We have a damson tree in the hedgerow and when the fruits are ripe and fall to the ground the damson stones are found in the droppings.

A friend Gerry, a biology lecturer, who lived on the south side of our village, attracted foxes to his patch consisting of a small conifer plantation and some grassland housing a tractor shed. An old gander lived in the open tractor shed shared by a vixen with an earth inside the shed. It was an astonishing sight to see the vixen pass the gander with a rabbit for her well-grown cubs dashing out to greet her for their supper. The cubs would argue about their share of the meal whilst the vixen would watch them from a distance, the goose was ignored by both cubs and mother.

Gerry and I decided that we would exchange information about the foxes that came to our different feeding stations, these were about a quarter of a mile apart. He was seeing around four different foxes during a night watch whilst at the other end of the village I was seeing up to five different foxes, I was able to sex as most of them had been coming since they were brought to the feeding station as cubs. The interesting findings we observed were that the foxes seen at the extreme ends of the village were distinctly separate social groups as we were able to identify and sex the individual animals. We carried out these observations a number of times to make sure that there was no interaction between the differing social groups of animals.

Foxes live in loose social groups where they may communicate by leaving signs such as scats, or urine, usually deposited on a prominent feature like a rock or a tree trunk. Acting as a scent marker, these are particularly noticeable during the breeding season, usually around January, when scent is being deposited throughout the territory. Each fox is able to observe the wanderings of other members of their social groupings and keep track of roaming individuals from other social groups.

In the breeding season there may have been some wanderings from strangers, particularly when a dominant dog fox may stray into another territory to investigate the availability of vixens in season.

In January 2012 I observed a dog fox not known to me enter the feeding station at around 9.30pm whilst my usual white-tipped dog and vixen were together. The stranger, a black – tipped dog fox, chased the resident dog fox away and the vixen climbed on top of a log pile and stayed there for several minutes. Later towards midnight the white-tipped dog fox returned and fed on the peanut bait.

Tracks and Scent Marking

Foxes, like most animals, stick to often well-marked tracks when moving around their territories. In the case of the fox, these tracks are usually narrower than badger tracks and often resemble a thin line often worn down to the bare earth especially when leading to or from an earth where cubs are present. The tracks are less well marked when the animal is on its feeding grounds as then foxes are moving randomly when hunting for voles, insects or earthworms. Crossing points such as a hedgerow or ditches often show a well-worn area where the animals jump across a ditch or pass through a hedge where traditionally generations of foxes have used these crossing points.

My late mother-in-law who lived within the precincts of the City of Nottingham had foxes passing through her garden nightly, there was a well-used earth in her neighbour's garden. The gardens were on a steep slope and at the very top of the garden there was a fox track leading from the nearby earth across her garden, this winding track was worn down to bare earth having been used by many generations of foxes. Urban foxes are sometimes described as inferior specimens to their country cousins, however, the town foxes I saw and photographed were fine looking animals, just as handsome as their rural counterparts.

Foxes have paired glands in the anus known as anal sacs which assist the animals to mark their territory with individual scats (droppings) carrying their scent, leaving a scent marker which in the mating season is quite pungent, and easily smelt by humans when close by.

Sometimes dog foxes will simply squat like a vixen and leave a drop of urine on the ground. Foxes when visiting usually check the deposits, these appear to be a signal indicating who has left them and how recently they have passed that way. Foxes also have a gland situated on the upper part of the tail a short way from where the tail is attached to the body. This shows up as a dark circular patch on the tail, there appears to be little known at present about the significance of this gland.

Although foxes appear to be rather smelly animals when we are fairly close by, there is no doubt that if the wind direction is blowing from a human to a fox, the fox will be able to smell us long before we can smell the fox.

Unlike badgers, where the animals live cooperatively in a sett maintaining the underground tunnels and chambers, foxes, apart from during the breeding season, are solitary animals living mainly on the surface, sleeping in dry ditches or broad hedgerows where they can curl up and sleep during their resting hours. Sometimes foxes will get off the ground and climb trees and rest there for the daytime hours. I have watched foxes climbing trees in early morning after a night's foraging. One Sunday as we lay in bed looking out onto permanent pasture grazed by sheep we saw a fox walk through the flock of sheep, circle a large beech tree and with a jump settle down in the lower branches of the tree and remain there until evening.

The sheep in this field took absolutely no notice of the fox as they were used to seeing foxes and the farmer told me of seeing a fox and a sheep nuzzling one another when checking his flock one morning. He also told

me that he had never lost a live lamb to a fox although he had seen a fox carrying a stillborn lamb from the same field. I have seen foxes in this field picking up lamb's testicles which become detached following the application of rubber bands applied by the farmer a similar thing happens when rubber rings are used to cut through the tails, sometimes the rubber rings show up in the scats of the foxes when they have been scavenging on these items.

On other occasions I have seen foxes jump across the edge of a pond which housed an old pollarded willow tree. The foxes would take a jump from the bank and appeared to put one leg into the water and land in the low pollarded branches then curl up to rest. Several times I tried to photograph a fox in the tree, approaching by following along a line of telegraph poles trying to conceal myself, but whenever I got anywhere near where the fox was lying up it would spot me. The fox would be resting with one eye open and seeing my approach would leap from the tree, make one splash in the water and make off to a nearby wood.

Foxes maintain contact with other members of their social group, probably other siblings and older family members such as maternal aunts, with the usual signals in the form of scats and urine but vocal signals are also of some significance.

Foxes make a variety of calls, scientists have identified more than two dozen different sounds but most of us will be familiar with the screams and barks made during the breeding season which peaks in January. Foxes seem to call at any time of the year, friends who live in the town seem to hear foxes calling more often than I hear them in open countryside. That may be because in the urban areas there are more foxes with smaller territories and there may be more need to reinforce the boundaries between social groups.

These calls are usually screams some people find distressing although I find them quite exciting. The other familiar call is a series of barks, sometimes three or more barks often described as yo-ho-ho calls. When very young, cubs make whining sounds, presumably when hungry or requiring some attention from the vixen.

When they are a little older and appearing above ground at about four – to six-weeks-old the sounds change into a clicking sound which seems to be a contact call made when cubs are beginning to wander away from the earth and are starting to become bolder. At this stage they are still staying together as a family, towards autumn they will become more independent of their parents and of each other, at this stage some of the male cubs may be chased out of the area by the more dominant foxes, usually a dominant dog fox which may be the father.

I have noticed that with an increase in organised game shooting in south Nottinghamshire there has been a decrease in the number of foxes seen at my feeding stations. I have heard very little in the way of calling between foxes in the breeding season, possibly because the foxes at low numbers

may not have such a need to keep in touch as there are fewer animals to contact.

A friend who has worked on an estate for around thirty years where an intensive type of game-keeping took place during recent years, has noticed fewer foxes calling during the breeding season. For some forty years there had been no shooting on this estate and there were three pairs of barn owls breeding there, as well as foxes, badgers, and more recently polecats have been recorded in the parkland. Several polecats run over on the busy road abutting the parkland. Some years ago this estate came under new ownership, with an introduction of intensive game shooting and the consequent reduction in the number of foxes. A number of traps and snares (some illegal) have been found in the woods and there was an increase in the illegal killing of badgers, the carcasses of several animals have been found on the rides and pastures.

Foxes regularly move in from the surrounding countryside to occupy traditional areas of what was a natural food supply, now being supplemented by a huge number of artificially reared, semi-tame, non-indigenous game birds. What carnivore could resist such a bonanza requiring little effort to catch?

Whilst some landowners and gamekeepers are aware of the various wildlife protection laws and observe them strictly, others take a different

attitude, consequently on some estates illegal snares have been found and poisons have also been used as well as illegal trapping and shooting. I visited many estates and farmers whilst carrying out work for the National Badger Surveys for various statuary bodies concerned with nature conservation. As a result of the survey work I spoke to many of the gamekeepers on the estates and discussed with them their duties as keepers and saw the methods of game rearing and those used for predator control.

Snaring is the most contentious way of taking predators such as foxes as this method is non-selective, often resulting in the catching of protected species such as badgers; these are powerful animals and usually suffer appallingly before succumbing.

Domestic animals such as cats and dogs can also be victims of snares and can suffer injuries or die unless found in good time. Although snares are supposed to be examined at least once every twenty-four hours, this is often ignored in some shoots where the keeper is part-time and has limited time for checking the devices. Once in Clipstone Forest in Nottinghamshire I was shown by a ranger the carcass of a fallow deer that had to be stalked and shot, it had a damaged hind leg that was trailing where it had been caught by a snare which was still attached.

Live cage traps are commonly used to take foxes and are baited using carrion as rabbits or birds such as wood pigeons. On one occasion I saw a large trout used as bait. Other methods include lamping from a vehicle using a high powered lamp attached to the vehicle roof or hand held lamps shining across the fields looking for the reflective shine from the eyes of the prey. Another method used by some keepers is to bait an area with carcasses of rabbits or some other carrion, then get off the ground with a high seat or wait in the branches of a suitable tree and shoot from there. One old gamekeeper I knew used this method and claimed to shoot dozens of foxes in a season.

Foxes had an earth in an old orchard abutting the pasture at the rear of our house, sometimes we would see a fox sunning itself lying close to a hedge. One old dog fox was often seen like this, he was largely ignored by the younger dog foxes, presumably he posed no threat to their territorial ambitions.

Sadly the old fox somehow got his forefoot caught in a snare and almost severed it at the ankle. He must have been close to starving as he was visiting us looking for food at any time of the day or night. I was able to borrow a feral dog cage trap and after a week of baiting the trap and leaving it un-sprung to get the animal used to entering the trap. I then sprung the trap one night and managed to catch him. I then called in an RSPCA inspector who humanely put him out of his suffering. The old fox was sheltered overnight in our garage in the trap and ate a meal during the night.

Breeding

As the breeding season approaches foxes start contacting each other as early as November and as I write this section in late December I have been watching a vixen at a feeding station where she is a nightly visitor. This fox was one of two that came as cubs last May, the other cub was a dog fox and left the area a few months ago. Recently when the young vixen is feeding I have seen a dog fox sitting watching her from a little way off. A few days ago I saw them both feeding together on the bait, on this occasion peanuts. They stayed together for a few minutes and the vixen who is smaller than the dog showed some mild aggression and the male moved away. I have seen this behaviour quite a few times over the years before the mating season proper, which normally takes place in January.

Pregnant vixens have been recorded as early as October. H.G.Lloyd mentions that a pregnant vixen killed on Boxing Day in 1962 was carrying cubs near full term and it was reckoned that she had mated in early to mid-October (H.G. Lloyd *The Red Fox*).

Vixens come into heat once a year and are only receptive to the males for a short time, reckoned to be around three days. Around this time they are followed by a number of males. There is usually much screaming and barking as the animals keep in contact with each other. There can also be a lot of fighting at this time especially amongst dog foxes when the more dominant fox is challenged. Occasionally foxes can kill a rival; I was once told by a member of an evening class I was taking that he had on a January evening witnessed two foxes fighting in his garden and the next morning he found one of the foxes dead in his pond. The pond was a shallow one so it unlikely that the fox had drowned accidentally.

Much scenting takes place during the breeding season, this is the time when foxes can be smelt strongly, especially if one is walking in the countryside or in urban areas when the scenting is most evident in and around large gardens. This is the time when foxes can be around in early evening or during daylight hours. I remember one January morning seeing four foxes running across the field opposite our house and then in the field at the back of the house. This was a vixen being pursued by three dog foxes. She must have become receptive and was going to be mated by one or more of the males. Sadly I did not on that occasion witness the mating, although I have seen this on several occasions in and around the same area.

On one occasion on the 17th of January I witnessed mating during the late afternoon in the field at the back of the house when the foxes became tied (as happens with domestic dogs). A friend telephoned in the evening of the same day having seen two pairs of foxes mating in a neighbouring parish. It appears that there was some kind of synchronisation of mating on that day in different locations. On another occasion I had foxes mating in the garden and tried to stalk them for a photograph. It was a freezing night and the frosty ground prevented a quiet approach causing the foxes to retreat into the pasture beyond the hedgerow.

The gestation period for vixens is around fifty-three days. Over the years I have seen heavily pregnant vixens at a feeding station, feeding almost until they are about to give birth. Once they have stopped coming to the feeding area I have been able to time them from when the cubs are expected to be born, to when they first leave the cubs, and their reappearance back at the feeding station after around eight weeks.

Well, before mating takes place vixens will have located a number of earths for when she is ready to produce her cubs. These may be earths she has already used in previous years, but can be newly dug, perhaps in part of a rabbit warren or in part of a badger sett not currently in use by the badgers. Other sites include dry drains or pipes, artificial earths as used by hunts, and as told to me by a local farmer, on top of a hay stack, which when being taken down revealed a family of fox cubs at the very top of the stack.

In the case of urban foxes many earths are found under garden sheds or are sometimes dug in the garden usually in shrubbery away from the house; in one case foxes dug an earth under a well-used pathway close to the house.

The cubs are born around the middle of March to early April or later in more northerly parts. They are covered with dark hair and are deaf and blind. Unlike badger cubs that are born into a cosy nest, fox cubs are born without nesting material on bare earth, the vixen staying with them for around two weeks, whilst the dog fox may bring in food for her. The excellent footage obtained from the BBC *Foxwatch* programme, with Steve Harris as adviser, showed a great deal of what goes on in an earth when the vixen gives birth and the dog fox's role in supplying the vixen with food in the early days. In this case the vixen gave birth to four cubs which is about the average number for a litter of cubs . Although this filming took place in an urban environment much of the behaviour would be typical in a rural situation.

Once their eyes and ears are open, which occurs at around two weeks, the cubs will crawl around the earth. Their eyes at this stage are blue in colour but later change to the amber colour found in adults, at around four to five weeks. At this stage the vixen will visit the cubs less frequently bringing in prey items such as voles and young rabbits or scavenged carrion, she can also produce regurgitated food for the cubs when they are being weaned.

Whilst watching badgers at a sett housing a family of fox cubs I have seen a vixen bring in a young rabbit at the same time each night for the cubs. She would look me in the eye whilst I was sitting on the ground in the wood near the sett, then walking past me she carried the rabbit to an entrance where the cubs would be waiting. Leaving the food for the cubs she would then retrace her steps, looking at me again as she went off through the woods. The vixen accepted me as did the badgers at the sett presumably because they had become habituated to my scent, and knew that I posed no threat to them. Whenever I took a stranger to watch the badgers or foxes, their normal cautious behaviour pattern would return and they became difficult to observe.

Vixens are known to act as aunts to cubs born for example to a relative who may have some difficulty in catering for her family because of circumstances. For instance a vixen may be run over or perhaps get lost in some other way. It is known for a relative perhaps a sister to take over the caring of the cubs.

I was once watching a fox family in an urban situation, the earth was under a large shed at the rear of a small garden, with a wall at the back of the shed with a steep drop down to a supermarket car park. The garden was bordered by fencing more than five feet high. The vixen would negotiate the fences at night to feed her five cubs, just about weaned when I first saw them. On my third visit to the fox family I was amazed to see not five but ten cubs all playing together. My conclusion was that there must have been another vixen with cubs nearby and on this occasion they probably came together as an extended family. Unfortunately I was not able to visit the foxes again, but the family with the earth in their garden confirmed that the original number of cubs in the litter was the five I saw on my first two visits.

The habit of a vixen moving her cubs to another location when disturbed was clearly shown when I was returning from a badger watch in the early hours of the morning. It was a dark night and very quiet, the village pub traffic having long departed. When I was approaching the pipe mentioned in the chapter on artificial badger setts, I could see in my headlights five small fox cubs playing in the road below the grass verge which housed the 30cm diameter pipe in the nearby ditch. When I was quite close to the cubs they scrambled onto the verge but this was too high for some of them to negotiate. Stopping the car I helped two of the cubs to negotiate the verge. All five cubs then disappeared into the pipe entrance.

The next day I examined the pipe and could see some of the cubs in the pipe. The ditch was lined with nettles and I had brought along a plastic bag to line the ditch whilst I lay on my stomach to view the pipe. I decided to try for a photograph of the cubs and in between passing traffic I lay down and focused my camera on the pipe entrance. After a while the cubs began to appear and I was lucky to get a couple of shots before they retired back into the safety of their artificial earth.

I went back to the pipe the next day but all seemed very quiet and looking into the earth I realised the scent I had left when lying in the ditch the previous day could have caused the vixen to remove her offspring to a safer location, but where? I knew where the nearest earth to the pipe was so I went two fields away to a pasture housing an old railway carriage. Under the carriage there was an old outlier badger sett consisting of two holes and sure enough a day or so later I saw the vixen sitting outside and cubs were playing under the carriage. How the vixen had moved the cubs I have no idea, had she carried them or did she lead them there?

Sometimes cubs can move with the guidance of the vixen. Once when returning from a session photographing bats being cared for by a woman in a neighbouring town, I was driving along a narrow road near home when I saw in the headlights what initially appeared to be a strange long animal crossing the road, on getting nearer I was delighted to see that it was a family of fox cubs crossing the road nose to tail. I stopped the car and the cubs went under a farm gate, I then got out and as the cubs disappeared their mother in the field opposite started to scream and give out a series of barks probably warning the cubs to take cover.

During the construction of a large storage area for coal at a now redundant colliery in south Nottinghamshire I was told of a family of fox cubs living in an earth in the huge pile of material which had been moved to make room for the coal stacking. The earth was situated between a canal path and was in the banking created by the colliery workings. When I first visited the earth I approached by way of the canal path and cautiously scaled the bank housing the earth, and as I peeped over the bank I was surprised to see a family of foxes consisting of a vixen and several cubs. The vixen on spotting me bared her teeth and then barked, warning her cubs to take cover, this they did by bolting into the earth. I knew that from now on I would need to take great care when next visiting the foxes as the cubs would now have an aversion to human scent having been warned by their mother to take cover.

Another occasion when a fox bared its teeth at me was at one of my feeding stations where some well-grown young foxes were feeding together, when an adult fox approached there was some aggression shown towards one of the cubs. I approached the scene and the adult fox ran off but the cub, which was lying on its back, bared its teeth briefly as I approached and then made off. The baring of teeth in this instance may have been a warning to another animal to back off or simply a signal indicating distress in a subdominant animal.

Cattle and sheep see foxes probably every night as a fox's territory would include most pastures grazed by farm animals, and as our house faces permanent pasture to the front and pasture to the rear I have seen many examples of fox and farm animal interaction over the last forty years. One interesting observation was a heifer chasing a fox around the margins of a field trying to prevent the fox entering an open barn where it would regularly lie up during daylight hours. The fox would access the barn by crossing the field of heifers. Most mornings the fox would return from its nightly foraging and make its way towards the barn, however, once the particular heifer spotted the fox it would charge up the field and prevent the fox from coming through the field. The fox would then try another

entrance and when the heifer saw it she charged again, eventually the fox would succeed and make the safety of the barn.

Contact with sheep is also an interesting topic, and although foxes in some areas are said to take lambs, I have never seen this although I once saw a fox take a stillborn lamb in the field opposite our house taking it to an earth a few hundred metres away. I have spoken to the farmer concerned and so far as he knows he has never lost a viable lamb to a fox, he also told me that he had once seen a fox nuzzling a lamb when checking his flock in the morning. In the same field I have often seen foxes pass through the flock and the sheep take absolutely no notice of the fox, although if it had been a dog or a number of dogs then the reaction of the sheep would have been very different as they instinctively recognise dogs as potential wolves from which they are of course descended.

Two other friends, both sheep farmers, have told me that so far as they know they have never lost a viable lamb to a fox. One of the farmers has his farm in the Lake District breeding the famous Herdwick sheep so favoured by Beatrix Potter. He has said that in forty years of sheep farming he has only lost one lamb that he couldn't account for. The other farmer friend along with his father had farmed sheep for fifty-seven years at the same location and had few losses that he could attribute to foxes.

The red fox is the only wild member of the dog family left in Britain since the last wolf was exterminated in the early eighteenth century in Scotland, and much earlier in the sixteenth century in England. Most conflict between foxes and dogs is deliberately created by man with dogs used to repel foxes from livestock or, more contentiously, dogs trained to pursue foxes as in fox-hunting and terrier work where small dogs such as the Jack Russell, Patterdale and Border terriers are bred to be able to enter earths and badger setts.

Foxes often encounter domestic cats, in my experience, the cat is nearly always dominant to the fox. I have once seen a vixen chase a cat away, this was when the vixen with a cub alongside her was sitting by a pond when a cat came through the hedgerow, immediately the vixen ran towards the cat and bowled it over. The vixen and the cub made off and a short time later the cat reappeared none the worse for the encounter. The majority of cat and fox meetings usually result in the fox backing off when confronted by a cat. I have seen on many occasions a fox retreat when a cat appears and takes the food intended for the fox. Not surprisingly dogs often retreat when faced with a cat they have cornered, especially when the cat stretches itself up snarling and hissing.

Hedgehogs are frequently present with the foxes at one of my feeding stations and are largely ignored by the foxes, although I have been told by a lady who runs an animal welfare centre that she has seen an injured hedgehog attacked by a fox. Most of the encounters I have seen between foxes and hedgehogs have been that the animals largely ignore each other especially when feeding together. On one occasion I have seen a fox carry out the classic vole leap when it heard a sound in the shrubbery and was painfully deceived when it landed on the back of a hedgehog, the poor fox made a rapid retreat when it realised its mistake.

Once I was able to witness a family of three foxes and five hedgehogs feeding on peanuts. The hedgehogs seemed to get the upper hand so far as the feeding was concerned as whenever a fox approached the peanuts one or more of the hedgehogs would flatten its body over the peanuts to make the food less accessible to the foxes.

The relationship between foxes and badgers is on the whole a mutual tolerance between the two animals as they are aware of each other's presence most of the time. They share the same habitat and are largely both crepuscular and nocturnal at different times in the season, so their paths will inevitably cross whilst out foraging. Occasionally the animals are sometimes foraging together when there is an abundant source of food attractive to both species, for example in the chapter on the badger I described both badgers and foxes which were seen in the same field feeding on the emerging daddy-long-legs.

When the badger and the fox were feeding together during the badger's stay with us, the fox would always defer to the badger when they came close together but there was no serious aggression. The badger is much bigger than the fox and is therefore the dominant animal. Whilst watching badgers at a local sett I saw a fox emerge from one of the entrances several times during the week, the fox usually exited the sett a few minutes before the first badger emerged but on one occasion the badger came out at exactly the same time as the fox was emerging from an adjacent tunnel, the badger growled and chased the fox away from the sett.

During severe weather, foxes will sometimes take shelter in part of a badger sett not currently used by the badgers. Whilst watching badgers at a large Leicestershire sett I saw two foxes emerge from an entrance and make off before the badgers emerged. The next evening I decided to try for a photograph and duly set up a camera to be fired remotely some distance from the entrance used by the foxes. Sure enough a fox emerged from the sett at exactly the same time as the previous night. I might have secured a picture but the fox emerged at full speed and was away before I could fire the shutter. Within a few moments the second fox emerged and this time I was ready and was able to get a photograph, although the fox looked nervous and clearly knew I was nearby.

I can cite other instances of foxes going into badger setts on a fairly regular basis during the hunting season. A landowner built, with advice from myself, an artificial badger sett in his woodland consisting of three underground chambers dug into the earth just inside the confines of the wood. The underground chambers were provided with drainage, access was provided by concrete pipes. Facility for the badgers to extend the sett was achieved by leaving some areas of bare earth under-ground, this would allow the animals to extend the sett naturally.

Originally badgers were brought from a wildlife collection in Derbyshire which was being closed down and they were put into the sett, these animals soon dispersed and at least one was soon a road casualty, however, badgers from a local sett soon took advantage of the facilities and the sett became active as it is to this day. The landowner was sympathetic towards hunting and allowed the huntsman to draw the wood for a fox but would not allow the sett to be blocked or permit terriers to be allowed underground. (Before the Hunting Act 2004, hunts were permitted to block badger setts, earths and drains to prevent the fox going to ground when being hunted). In the case of the artificial sett the owner told me that many times after the hunt had left the area he would creep up to the sett and often saw a fox lying in an entrance to the sett facing outwards. This confirmed to me what I had always suspected that no fox under normal conditions would ever enter a chamber of an active sett if a badger were present. Foxes do enter setts and, as has been mentioned, can sometimes rear a family of cubs there, but they are using the parts of the sett not currently used by the badgers.

There has been little hunting in the parish I live in, two of the biggest farmers in the area wouldn't allow the hunt onto their land so they rarely met in the village.

A Lucky Fox

On one occasion a Leicestershire hunt met in a neighbouring village and put up a fox, chasing it along the road into our village. The fox was lucky because a lady solicitor who lived on the road near the heart of the village saw the fox being pursued by the hounds and mounted followers and quickly opened her garage door. The fox took advantage of this chance opportunity and took refuge in the garage. The door was quickly closed behind the fox, an altercation then took place between the lady of the house and the huntsman who demanded his fox. A certain amount of impolite language was exchanged and eventually the hunt rode off in the direction from where they came. Later that evening I was called by the fox's saviour and asked if I would help release the fox.

When I opened the garage door I was met with a clearly distressed animal that was lying on the bench amid a pile of timber. I then took a photograph of the fox which was reluctant to leave. Using a yard brush I gently pushed the animal off the bench. Once out of the garage the fox dashed off into the night going off in the direction from where it had been chased.

Over the years I have seen dozens of foxes at my home feeding station

and several have clearly recognised me and have responded accordingly. One vixen would in the evening sit in the grass field at the back of the house and when I noticed her and called she would come right up to the house. I would call "sit" to her and hold my hand up whereupon she would sit just like our dog and I would be able to take photographs.

Another young dog fox would come very early in the evening and have a good scratch, yawn and then wander around the garden. I could follow this fox who would behave perfectly normally, caching food and scenting around the garden. I had never tried to tame this fox, from when it first appeared it just seemed unfazed by us, and would have entered the house had we allowed it. This particular fox clearly recognised us as one afternoon I was walking my dog down a green lane when I looked across a field and saw a cage trap baited with rabbit and pheasant carcasses where a fox was sitting upright in the trap.

I decided to investigate and upon seeing my dog the fox panicked and was obviously distressed.

I took the dog some distance from the trap and tied her up and then went back to the trap, as I approached the fox came to the entrance of the trap and I lifted the cage trap door. The fox left the trap and sat on the side of a ditch looking towards me. I realised that the fox knew me and it was the fox visiting us most evenings. I collected my dog and walked home.

Shortly after arriving home I was amazed to see the fox come through the hedge into the garden and stay for a few minutes before moving away. Was I wrong to rescue the fox? I believe that such an intelligent animal as this particular fox deserved to survive and as an indigenous animal it was to me far more interesting than any non-indigenous game birds.

In 1959 whilst working with silver foxes (a variation of the red fox) appearing to show a degree of empathy with humans, a Russian scientist Dmitri Balyaer observed that some foxes were more tolerant of humans than others. From this he began choosing these foxes for selective breeding and eventually produced a number of foxes that were rather different in behaviour from their wild counterparts. These foxes were behaving rather like dogs, wagging their tails and responding to commands such as "sit" and were retrieving objects and performing other commands. They also began to come into season every six months instead of annually like their wild brethren. By the third generation the selected foxes were producing offspring that were showing considerable degrees of tameness, by the eighth generation the tameness had increased and by the fortieth generation were as tame as any domestic dog. In 1996 there were around 700 foxes domesticated, but without adequate funding for the project their numbers had declined to around 100 animals in 1998. Balyaer died in 1985 and his work continued under Lyudmila Trut who had worked with him on the original experiments that are continuing to this day. Sadly the experiments

are at a much lower level than before because of funding problems, some of the funding comes from the sale of the tame foxes as pets.

I often wonder if the fox who regularly visited us and allowed us to follow it around the garden would have been a suitable candidate for a similar taming programme as the Balyaer

Experiments? This animal certainly behaved in a very different way to any other of the foxes I have met with over the last 40 years.

The late Eric Ashby, a naturalist who lived in the New Forest, kept a number of foxes, many were rescued or orphaned animals. Eric also filmed badgers and foxes in the wild. Some of the first pictures taken underground of badgers were taken by Eric and were shown in television programmes. Many people visited Eric at his sanctuary and were enchanted by the behaviour of the foxes. Schoolchildren were especially delighted to be able to interact with the animals in perfect safety. Many of Eric's foxes were able to return to the wild and would often revisit the sanctuary, many months, sometimes even years after they had been encouraged to return to their natural state.

The Wildcat *(Felis silvestris)*

The only native member of the family *Felidae* (the cat family) in Britain, the wildcat is probably the most endangered of our carnivores. Although once widespread throughout the British Isles, it was severely persecuted, largely by gamekeepers, in the past and reduced to its present status of being confined to the Highlands of Scotland. There it is threatened not only by man but by its association with the domestic cat of which there are estimated to be around eight million kept as pets and some living wild as feral cats. Unless neutered, these feral cats breeding in the wild with the genuine wildcat is a serious threat to the genetic make up of the latter animal. The estimation of the numbers of truly wild cats is variable, some think that there are no truly wild cats left, genetics are perhaps the only way of confirming this or otherwise. Hopefully the true wild cat is still out there and holding its

own but there are serious threats to the truly wild animals as mentioned earlier.

Historical records of wildcats exist until the 1800s when it was reported to be present in Wales, northern England and Scotland. Previously the wildcat was to be found throughout Britain in forested areas, including my home county of Nottinghamshire where it was recorded at Worksop in 1586 and in the village of Cuckney in 1732 (Lovegrove 2007). Large numbers of wildcat killings took place in Devon and Cornwall where some ninety-

two were paid for in parish records at St Neots and in another ten parishes thirty-seven were killed up to 1711. In Devon 311 were killed between 1629 and 1699, mainly in the parish of Hartland.

An example of a possible hybrid cat is the so called Kellas cat which was revealed by a gamekeeper who shot a black cat in or near the village of Kellas in Morayshire in Scotland from where the beast gets its name. There is much scepticism about the black cat and some believe this cat is simply a melanistic version of the domestic cat (*Felis catus*). I have photographed a captive Kellas cat at the Wildlife Park near Kingussie in Scotland, this shows the black colouration and similarity of posture with the genuine wildcat. I have also taken pictures of genuine wildcats held in the same park showing the tabby coat of the wild animal and the large black tip to the tail.

Whilst staying in Scotland at Nethybridge in the Cairngorms as mentioned in the chapter on badgers, I contacted the Canadian field scientist Paul Latour who was working on badger studies for Dr Hans Kruuk. Paul told me he had seen a female wildcat with two kittens in the hills behind Loch Pityoulish and one night when out with him following the badgers we heard a tremendous scream. Paul said that this was the call of a wildcat, which he had heard on a number of occasions. I have never heard the call since but hope one day to revisit and perhaps hear the exciting scream again.

Once I was given some information of otters feeding on a river during daylight hours and set off for the location with some enthusiasm. On the way we drove along a road littered with the carcasses of road casualty rabbits. Looking to the woodland slope on our right I noticed what looked like a badger sett and saw a white flash at an entrance. Thinking it might be a badger, I parked the car and made my way to the area. I walked up the slope and was amazed to see what appeared to be a pair of kittens peeping from the entrance. They were pure white but not albinos as the eyes were not of a reddish colour but were of a yellowish hue. These kittens appeared to be undomesticated as they were spitting and snarling as they retreated backwards down the tunnel when I approached.

Thinking there must be a female in the area I decided to wait for the mother to return hoping for a wildcat to appear. After a long wait and nothing happening I decided on another approach. Going back to the road I collected one of the numerous dead rabbits lying there and attaching it to a piece of string went back to the den. After setting up the camera, I carefully lowered the rabbit slowly down the entrance where the kittens were showing earlier. Slowly pulling up the string I was delighted to see both kittens following the bait to the surface and managed to take a couple of pictures before the kittens managed to take the rabbit underground. I have not been able to establish the status of the kittens but they were extremely wild in their behaviour. It was an interesting experience but I never got to see the otters.

When staying in the Cairngorms I have driven around the forests at night using a powerful night light and believe I have seen wildcats on these drives crossing the rides. I also believe I have seen the real animal on the Morvern peninsula whilst staying in a cottage by a sea loch. One night I baited a spot in the heather close to a window and set up a camera and flash in one of the windows. First red deer came down from the hills to feed on the more succulent grasses and when they had drifted away into the night, sure enough a wild looking cat came to feed on the baited area on a couple of occasions. I managed to take a few pictures and hoped one would be in focus.

Wildcats prefer a woodland habitat, and after the extensive period of persecution the Forestry Commission probably helped recovery, assisting the spread of the animals with their extensive plantations. Young plantations are often favoured as they have dense coverage of heather or grasses often containing large populations of mice and voles as well as rabbits. Wildcats

usually have their dens within the woods often in the rocky outcrops or within the many gaps found within the rock falls. They can utilise deserted badger setts or old fox earths, and rest amongst the hollows beneath old tree roots. Their preferred habitat may consist of areas of rough grassland bordering woodlands or the un-grazed edges of fields containing cover suitable for rabbits or hares and small mammals. Wildcats now have a number of organizations concerned for their future which monitor and record their presence. They now have legal protection and are included within Schedule 5 of the Wildlife and Countryside Act 1981.

Feeding

The food of wildcats is rather like that of foxes, whatever is available is taken, from rabbits and hares to small mammals such as voles and mice. Shrews are taken and eaten although they have scent glands along the underbelly, these are said to deter most predators. Birds, fishes, reptiles and amphibians are all part of the diet. Smaller invertebrate prey items such as insects are also eaten and some carrion is taken such as sheep carcasses (many sheep and lambs die naturally in the hills, especially in the springtime) or road kills such as rabbits. Some game birds may be taken but a study in Scotland (Hewer R.1983) comparing the food of foxes and wildcats showed that game birds were not high on the list in the cat's diet.

The marking of a territory or home range (the area within the territory occupied by an individual animal) is carried out by deposition of urine or faeces at prominent sites on a boulder or other features such as a tree trunk.

When depositing faeces the wildcat usually leaves the dropping in the open, unlike the domestic cat that digs a small pit filling it in after use.

Males are said to carry out much more territorial marking than the females, spraying urine at or about the nose level of a female cat on tree trunks or other natural objects, thus leaving a message that he is in the area. Male cats have a much larger range than the females and may overlap a number of female home ranges thus ensuring that their genes are spread widely.

Breeding

Wildcats usually mate early in the year from January to March, the females are in oestrus from five to eight days when the males pursue them. Successful mating is followed by a gestation period of sixty-six days when the kits are born. When first born the young are furred but blind, the eyes opening after eight to thirteen days. The eye colour changes from blue at five months to a golden colour at around seven months of age. After two months the kittens have a full set of milk teeth. Female wildcats produce one litter in early spring unlike domestic or feral cats, which can produce a litter of kits at any time of the year.

The future of the true wildcat depends entirely on humans fostering a tolerant attitude towards wildlife of all species, and especially towards those which are critically endangered such as the magnificent beast of the Highlands, hopefully by dealing with the dilution of the gene pool by preventing the spread of feral cats and wherever possible catching and neutering these animals. The fostering of a more tolerant attitude by gamekeepers towards the wildcat would be helpful to their future.

Insectivores

The three families found in the British Isles in the Orders *Erinaceomorpha and Soricomorpha* are hedgehogs, shrews and the mole, although moles are absent from Ireland. Hedgehogs are the largest animals in this grouping and belong to the family *Erinaceidea* and are the only representative of this family in Britain.

The Hedgehog (*Erinaceus europaeus*)

The Hedgehog is familiar to everyone and popularly represented in children's books and was featured in Beatrice Potter's books as Mrs Tiggywinkle. There are a number of local bodies involved with caring for hedgehogs, whether injured or in trouble for any other reason, and an after-care programme before release into the wild at suitably selected sites.

Nationally there is the British Hedgehog Preservation Society (BHPS) giving advice on hedgehogs and their conservation, currently with a membership of around 11,000. There is also a wildlife hospital known as Tiggywinkles, this cares for a variety of injured or orphaned animals as well as hedgehogs. With an estimated decline in numbers of some 25% over the last decade, the hedgehog is certainly in need of all the help we can offer, to arrest, and hopefully reverse its decline in the future.

The hedgehog is one of only three species of mammals in Britain which hibernate during the winter months in Britain, the other two being the bats and the common dormouse.

To hibernate, hedgehogs have to build up their body fat in the autumn months to prepare for a prolonged period of cold weather tucked up as they usually are, in a carefully prepared nest in a dry hedgerow or a shrubby part of a garden where I have sometimes found them. Unless the animals have sufficient fat to take them through a cold spell, they are compelled to continue feeding. Two kinds of fat are produced, a white fat stored in and around the body which is used up during hibernation and a so-called brown fat stored around the shoulders which assists the animal to warm up during waking periods. During mild spells in the winter months, hedgehogs will sometimes stir from their deep sleep and visit an obviously remembered source of food. In the case of my garden, peanuts are fed to attract foxes that often feed alongside hedgehogs during the summer time, however, I have

in winter seen hedgehogs come to feed on the peanuts even when there is snow on the ground and the temperature is below zero.

One winter we saw two very small hedgehogs from a late litter feeding on peanuts left out for the foxes, and we decided to see if we could get them through the winter without the bother of taking them into captivity as they would not have the stored body fat to cope with hibernation. We fed with small pieces of liver and chicken as well as the usual supply of peanuts the youngsters which appeared nightly as regular as clockwork, who seemed to thrive and would continue to visit the food source at temperatures well below zero, even with snow on the ground. The success story is that we were able to get them through the winter months and into spring when they fed normally along with the other visitors such as the foxes and other hedgehogs.

Feeding

Natural food consists of insects of various kinds as well as earthworms and caterpillars and a host of other invertebrates and of course slugs. Often the remains of beetles can be seen in the droppings of hedgehogs especially the *elytra* or wing parts of insects which show up well, often on the surface of the dropping. Droppings are deposited randomly throughout their territory and can also be found on lawns, paths and patios. Like most animals the droppings reveal much of the food intake of the animal and hedgehog droppings are useful for analysing the variety of different food sources of the animal, although it can be a messy business breaking down the droppings and separating the remains of the prey items.

Breeding

After emerging from hibernation, male hedgehogs are capable of mating in early springtime and females can be pregnant from early May to late September. Early spring mating can result in four to six young being born in early June after a gestation period of around four-and-a-half to five weeks. Later mating can result in a second litter being born as late as the end of September. The young of these later litters are the vulnerable generation needing to feed well if they are to build up sufficient body fats to enable them to go into hibernation. Without the build-up of the body fats these late born youngsters are unlikely to survive the winter months unless they are taken into care and fed during this time. It is to the credit of the many care centres that often take in some of these late-born hedgehogs where they grow and survive through to springtime when many of them can be released back into the wild in a suitable environment.

Hedgehogs are not very vocal animals so far as communication is concerned. A number of sounds can be heard but these are mainly to do with feeding or mating. Scent seems to be an important form of communication. I have watched hedgehogs feeding and then moving on whereupon another hedgehog has come onto the lawn and immediately started running around following the scent tracks of the earlier animals and apparently trying to locate them. Whilst watching three hedgehogs feeding on the lawn recently a fourth animal appeared and immediately began pushing one of the smaller animals around aggressively. Several times it managed to get its nose under the belly and tip the small animal onto its side where it remained for a few minutes before slowly righting itself when the aggressive one resumed the attack repeating the assault several times during the next hour.

This behaviour may be when a dominant male meets with another male. Aggressive action was also seen when one of two small hedgehogs attacked the other grasping it by the finer hair near the face and shaking it rather like a dog with a toy. When a female is in season the male will circle the female emitting a loud snorting sound. At this time it is possible to creep towards the animals and get fairly close to them before they scent you and run off into the night.

When they are feeding one can sometimes hear them making a low-pitched snuffling sound as they search for their prey. The loudest noise I have heard from a hedgehog was when a horse grazing in the pasture at the rear of our former house trod upon one. There was a high pitched squeal and upon investigating the noise I found the unfortunate animal flattened across the back, and of course dead. This incident would be rare, unlike the many other causes of mortality in the hedgehog population.

The motor car is the major cause of mortality. However, should a badger meet a hedgehog whilst out foraging and the badger is sufficiently hungry then there is no defence in the hedgehog's armoury that could deter the badger from a substantial meal. A badger with its powerful claws would soon scrub open the soft belly parts of the hedgehog and consume the unfortunate animal leaving the skin turned inside out.

Over a number of years we have had badgers visit our garden and as described in an earlier chapter one animal has stayed with us for several months. One night I saw two hedgehogs foraging in the garden and later saw a badger feeding near the compost heaps. The next morning on looking

out of the landing window I could make out the shape of an animal at the bottom of the garden. When I investigated the supposed animal I saw the freshly turned out skin of a hedgehog and was in no doubt that one of the hedgehogs I had seen the previous evening had finished up inside the badger and the badger had left the outside of the hedgehog lying near the compost heap.

Foxes must meet with many hedgehogs during their nightly wanderings and I see them both on a nightly basis when they visit my feeding station. Over forty years of intensive watching of both hedgehogs and foxes I have never seen a fox attack a hedgehog, except by mistake as mentioned in the chapter on foxes. However, I have no doubt that a fox would attack a weakened hedgehog and speaking with people who run a hedgehog rescue facility I have been told that when they attempt to release hedgehogs with some disability these animals are sometimes attacked by foxes.

Foxes certainly take hedgehogs and other victims of the motor car that have suffered their demise as road casualties, as do badgers, crows, rooks, magpies and a host of other scavengers. These scavengers are helping to keep our roads clean of the carcasses that would otherwise have to be collected by local authorities and be paid for out of our taxes

The Mole *(Talpa europaea)*

Although moles are rarely seen above ground being fossorial or largely underground tunnel dwellers, few people would fail to recognise the animal from the many representations used as illustrations in children's literature and of course one of the main characters in Kenneth Grahame's classic book *Wind in the Willows.*

Although distributed throughout the mainland of Britain and on some islands the mole is absent from Ireland. Few people have seen the animal in the flesh so to speak that is of course because of the mole's specialised way of life, spending the majority of its time underground patrolling the elaborate tunnel system in search of food and defending its territory against intruders. Moles do, however, sometimes come above ground in search of prey items in wet weather and are taken as food by predators such as foxes and tawny owls as well as herons which have been observed waiting near mole hills and taking surfacing animals. I have seen the almost complete remains of a mole in a tawny owl pellet deposited on a gatepost although that would have been taken during the night.

The mole is perfectly adapted for its subterranean way of life being wedge-shaped with a pointed highly sensitive nose and sensitive whiskers. The powerful forelegs are well adapted for digging and the fur is soft and does not lie in the usual mammal pattern from head to tail, but is short and when touched feels silky, and is able to be moved in any direction, thus the mole can reverse in its tunnel without resistance from its *pelage.* The tail is short and usually carried upright. The eyes are very tiny but are visible when seen close up. These organs are probably capable of detecting bright light or strange shapes, but good eyesight would be of no great advantage to an animal spending most of its life underground in total darkness. There are no visible ear flaps but the concealed ears are capable at least of detecting loud and sudden noises.

There are a number of colour variations in the pelage from albino to a pinkish type found in the Newstead area of Nottinghamshire. These seem to persist in mole populations more than in surface-living mammals, probably because moles are for the most part not as easily predated upon as are surface-dwelling mammals such as mice and rabbits which, when bearing a light coat, are easily detected by predators.

Moles need to search for water on the surface in dry conditions and are sometimes killed by dogs, our springer spaniel dog when taken for walks in the summer months often used to return carrying a mole after a run alongside a cornfield. These animals must have been on the surface as they were easily taken within minutes of the dog being released from her lead.

Once when I was watering the garden, I forgot to turn off the tap causing the freely flowing water to flood under the garden shed. When I realised I had left the tap on I returned to the garden and was surprised to see a mole appear from under the shed having been flooded out of its home. However, I have only once seen a molehill in our current garden situated in open country, whereas at our previous home that was also was in the countryside, we frequently had molehills appearing on the lawn.

Most people will have seen molehills especially on pastures, and with patience one can determine in which direction the mole is moving by watching for movement on freshly excavated mounds and then looking out for the next mound being pushed up indicating the way the underground tunnels are progressing. Sometimes one can estimate the extent of the underground tunnel system by following the molehills as they spread out over a pasture, these being the workings of a single animal. Sometimes shallow tunnelling can be seen near the surface of the land on pastures or in woodland where the mole is feeding near to the surface. Moles will have a nest within the tunnel system where the animal can rest between the periods of feeding. Females also use the nests to produce their young. Material lining the nest usually will be of local dried grasses or leaves. Sometimes a larger than usual mound will appear, especially on low lying ground, these are known as fortresses, they can contain several layers of tunnels and a nest area.

The purpose of the tunnels is to collect food, usually earthworms, but also any invertebrate animal such as beetles or grubs which may fall into the tunnel system and be taken by the mole as it traverses the tunnels every three or four hours. Worms are sometimes stored in small side excavations after being disabled by biting the head end, thus preventing the worm from crawling away. This forms a kind of larder where prey items are kept until required.

During very dry periods worms go deep down and often gather together, sometimes in a knot to avoid dehydration, thus making them more difficult to locate. It is likely that, when the worms are deep down during drought periods, that moles may be driven onto the surface to seek their food. Earthworms are the single most important item in the diet of the mole and can count for as much as 90% of the diet during the late summer until the spring period. During the summer months insect larvae are taken more frequently along with slugs, snails and millipedes.

Little is known about the breeding activity of moles as mating takes place underground. It is uncertain whether a female will tolerate a number of males or be receptive to a single male. The breeding season takes place in spring when, after a gestation period of four weeks, a litter on average consists of four young born naked and blind. After around two weeks fur begins to grow and they continue to be fed by their mother's milk for around a further two weeks. After around five weeks the young make exploratory forays around the nest area. Around seven weeks of age the young are probably evicted from their mother's territory and have to seek their own

territories from above ground making them at this stage vulnerable to predation.

Man's relationship with the mole has been a fractious one especially so far as agriculture is concerned. From being a woodland animal the mole has with forestry clearance moved into the areas turned into pasture or arable farmland. Because of the large numbers of earthworms found on these fertile areas the mole's activity is seen in the series of molehills. Moles can cause havoc in gardens with their digging activities and are a problem on golf courses where mounds can cause havoc with games. I have managed to deter moles in one of my gardens by watching for their digging activity and moving ahead of their digging and beating the ground with the flat blade of a spade several times heavily on the ground sending the moles scurrying back to the farmland pasture where they originated.

In times of more traditional farming methods, professional mole catchers existed in some villages and travelled to farms requiring their services. They were paid per mole caught and made extra income by selling the skins, these were turned into jackets and trousers. Moles are still trapped and killed in large numbers and various traps are manufactured for the purpose. In recent times there has been a resurgence of professional mole catchers, probably due to the banning of the use of the poison strychnine in 2006. Various organisations represent modern mole catchers and there are a lot of operators advertising their services which can be seen online or in the pages of various agricultural magazines.

In spite of the nuisance factor, moles are fascinating animals of which much remains to be discovered, especially about their underground way of life. This is difficult to study with usual methods such as live trapping techniques. Studies made above ground can still provide some information about their behaviour patterns. No doubt science in the future will enable observations to be made of the underground activities of this fascinating but largely unseen member of our native fauna.

Shrews (*Soricidae*)

Three species of shrew are found throughout the mainland of Britain; the common shrew, the pygmy shrew and the water shrew. Another shrew, the lesser white-toothed shrew, is found within the British Isles only on the islands of Scilly and in the Channel Isles.

All our shrews belong to the order *Soricamorpha* and are mainly insect eaters. Worms, woodlice and other small invertebrates are taken by the larger species. Earthworms are not eaten by pygmy shrews. The water shrew includes in its diet aquatic prey such as frogs, newts and small fish. Crustaceans such as water shrimps (*Gammarus*) and the water-louse (*Asellus*) are also taken and are probably more important in the diet than vertebrate species.

All our shrews are active throughout the twenty-four hours and in between frantic periods of feeding short rest periods are taken. Shrews need to consume around 80% to 90% of their body weight in order to survive. This high rate of activity continues for every month of the year.

The Water Shrew (*Neomys fodiens*)

The water shrew is the largest of the three species found on mainland Britain and is distinguished by its dark fur, appearing blackish from a distant with a whitish underbelly. The ears are hidden in the fur and the tail is fringed below with short stiff hairs and is used like a rudder when swimming underwater. As the name implies this shrew is mainly found near clean rivers and streams. Water shrews are not found exclusively close to a watercourse but can sometimes be found well away from running water. We have in our garden two ponds containing two species of newts as well as other amphibians but have never seen a water shrew in the ponds. I have, however, found over a number of years two water shrews under corrugated tins put out for grass snakes to bask under, as well as the other two mainland species the common shrew and the pygmy shrew.

Many years ago whilst taking Workers Educational Association (WEA) classes on British Mammals in the Mansfield area of Nottinghamshire I asked the class if they knew of a clean stream in the area which might be suitable for water shrews, as a result a clean stream in Pleasley Vale was chosen. A field visit was arranged and we met at the site and set off downstream looking for sightings of the animals. To my astonishment and I think that of the rest of the party we had only travelled a short distance when we all witnessed a water shrew dive into the stream and with air trapped in its fur, its silvery body began hunting for prey near the bank. After a short time the shrew emerged and shook itself and consumed its catch, this appeared to be a small crustacean. The shrew then cleaned itself and dived into the stream to seek out another prey item. Wandering further downstream we came across another water shrew hunting the waterside and occasionally diving into the water. We all appreciated the sighting of the water shrews. Unfortunately shortly after the field trip, a colliery spoil heap on the opposite side of the road to the stream became flooded and some of the slurry was carried across the road and into the stream where we had witnessed the shrews feeding.

I am told that the clean stream we had visited became polluted and most of the aquatic life was destroyed. I have not visited the area for a number of years but hope that the stream has cleared up and the shrews may be enjoying a clean environment once more.

The Common Shrew (*Sorex aranaeus*)

Although the common shrew is as the name implies one of our commonest small mammals it is often seen dead rather than alive as it lives mainly in the leaf litter and in the tunnels of other animals such as wood mice and voles. Dead specimens are sometimes seen on tracks in woodlands as well as paths in nature reserves and are regularly found in gardens especially rural ones. Like all shrews, common shrews are territorial and are sometimes seen fighting, possibly over territory. In spring when the shrews are courting they are tolerant of each other giving us a chance of observing them in their frantic activities.

Because of their active lives shrews only tend to live between one and one-and-a-half years. Shrews need to feed every few hours throughout the twenty-four hours and can easily succumb if deprived of food for a few hours. When live trapping for small mammals, traps using an escape hole need to be provided to allow the shrews to escape. Although common, all the British shrews are protected under Schedule 6 of the Wildlife and Countryside Act 1981 and a licence is required to catch or handle shrews.

Pygmy Shrew (*Sorex minutus*)

The pygmy shrew as the name suggests is the smallest of our mainland shrews and consequently seeks out smaller prey items than the other two species, usually eating small beetles, woodlice, flies and their larvae, spiders and bugs. Unlike the other two common mainland species the pygmy shrew is also found throughout Ireland.

All three shrews breed two or three times a year starting in spring, usually around April with a gestation period of three to three-and-a-half weeks. Late litters are born in August or September, and the young number between three and nine according to species, water shrews probably having the smallest litters.

Shrews are predated on by barn owls, tawny owls and kestrels, as well as foxes, cats, and small carnivores, such as stoats and weasels. Some are eaten and their remains have been found in the droppings of mammals and the pellets of barn owls and less commonly tawny owls. Lots are killed by cats but are left uneaten possibly because of the scent glands found on the flanks, or in the case of water shrews it is believed that they stun their prey with venom produced with the saliva, this may also be a deterrent to predators.

Rodents (*Rodentia*)

We have in Britain fifteen species of rodent, around seven of which have been introduced by the hand of man. Unlike all the other species of British mammals, rodents have a single pair of incisor teeth in the lower and upper jaw. These grow throughout life and there is a gap between the incisors and the molar teeth known as the diastemic gap.

Five families are classified now that the beaver (*Castor fiber*) has been re-introduced into at least two areas of Britain. These introductions are largely experimental but escapees are likely to result in wild free-living animals. Beavers are native to Britain but became extinct through hunting and other forms of persecution as long ago as the twelfth century.

Squirrels (*Sciuridae)*

This family is familiar to everyone who has seen the ubiquitous grey squirrel (*Sciurus carolinensis*) or our native red squirrel *(Sciurus vulgaris)* is well known to readers of Beatrice Potter as Squirrel Nutkins. Sadly the introduction of the grey squirrel to Britain in the latter half of the eighteenth century has impacted on our native red squirrel, causing the native red to become the rarer of the two species.

Introductions of the grey squirrel were recorded in 1876 when T.V. Brocklehurst released a pair in Henbury Park in Cheshire. A pair of grey squirrels shot at Highfields in Nottinghamshire in 1884, were possibly released in the area but may have originated from the Cheshire introductions. Since the original introductions in 1876 several other introductions from the USA have been made in England and Wales and also into Scotland from a Canadian source. The animals were also introduced into Ireland in County Longford in 1911.

Grey Squirrel *(Sciurus carolinensis)*
Red Squirrel (*Sciurus vulgaris)*

The grey squirrel is the larger of the two species weighing in at around 480g to 600g depending on season, compared to the red squirrel's 260g to 285g, the heavier weights being achieved in the autumn months when feeding is plentiful. Grey squirrels also develop a reddish tinge in the summer sometimes causing them to be mistaken for red squirrels.

Grey squirrels spend more time on the ground than our native red squirrel and tend to be able to find a greater variety of food than reds although both species eat the seeds of coniferous trees such as pine, larch and spruce. The grey squirrel also eats acorns and the catkins of the oak tree, as well as the seeds of several other deciduous trees including beech, hornbeam, sycamore and where available, elm. The outer bark of trees are sometimes stripped off, to reveal the soft under-bark which oozes sap and helps the squirrels to get through the winter months.

When food is plentiful squirrels will take food some distance from the source and bury it (caching) using their forepaws to excavate a hole, and then cover over the seed to conceal it from other rodents. They detect the buried food source by scent but often fail to recover all the buried seeds. Some of the undetected seeds, particularly acorns, may then go on to germinate and help to sustain our deciduous forests.

Both species of squirrel build nests called dreys, to rest and sleep in, and to provide a safe and secure home to breed in. The nests of grey squirrels are usually built in the upper branches of deciduous trees and are usually of two kinds, one a more temporary structure for resting in and a more substantial one for breeding in. The more permanent nests are usually lined with fine material such as grass, moss or bark for heat retention and a waterproof outer layer of twigs. Grey squirrels will also use large holes in tree trunks and are known to enter the roofs of houses. In the case of a friend who lives in an old farmhouse, grey squirrels found an entrance into the roof space where they would no doubt have bred had he not trapped them and prevented their re-entry by cutting down the ivy which the squirrels were using to access the roof space.

Red squirrels build their nests mostly from material from pines or other cone-bearing trees from which seasonally they gather cones and other edible material, but they have been recorded as nesting in a church tower as well as sometimes nesting at ground level in hollow fallen trees.

Both red and grey squirrels have two periods of breeding, one in winter (January – March) and the second later on in summer in June or July, or sometimes as late as September. Three young are born on average to both species after a gestation period of thirty-eight days in the case of the red and forty-four days in the case of the grey squirrel. The young are born naked and blind and are totally dependent upon their mother, the father taking no part in the youngster's welfare. When the young are three weeks old they develop a short fuzzy fur and soon after their eyes and ears open. The youngsters then start to grow their teeth and start to chew twigs inside the nest.

Female squirrels will sometimes move their young from one nest site to another and I remember seeing a female squirrel doing just that on a visit to Bradgate Park in Leicestershire. I was there photographing the deer when I noticed a grey squirrel approaching where I was standing. It was a female who was carrying a youngster by the loose skin on the back. The youngster was taken up a tree in which there was a drey, where the mother left the youngster, and the process was repeated with another two youngsters. The young squirrels appeared to have a covering of fur but the eyes appeared to be closed. I presumed the mother squirrel may have been disturbed and was perhaps moving the youngsters to a safer place. A radio-tagged female squirrel is reported to have moved her young three times during their infancy, finishing up at their original nest site.

When they are about seven weeks old, the young squirrels start exploring their surroundings and, as with most mammals, spend a lot of time playing and following their mother around, learning where the food sources are and discovering their home range. Around ten weeks of age they will become weaned and their mother's visits to the nest become less

frequent. The young at this time are becoming independent of their mother and they are foraging for themselves. Eventually they will move out and separate and find their own territory and construct a nest for themselves.

In their heyday the red squirrel was found widely throughout Britain, in my home county of Nottinghamshire there are records of the animals being present within living memory. A friend Richard Wadkin, a retired sheep farmer who farmed for many years at Widmerpool in Nottinghamshire, told me of a colony of red squirrels in and around the churchyard in that parish which he observed as a boy in the 1920s. Landowner and farmer, the late Myles Hildyard of Flintham Hall, Nottinghamshire, also told me of the presence of red squirrels in and around the Flintham estate in the 1920s

The red squirrel at one time was regarded as a pest in forestry and large numbers were killed because of damage to trees. There were a number of squirrel clubs who went out and shot red squirrels. One such club operated in the New Forest and in 1880 was reported to have shot up to 2,200 squirrels each year. Established in 1903 in Scotland the Highland Squirrel Club is reported to have shot 82,000 red squirrels in its first thirty years shooting on a number of Highland estates. Other reports of the destruction of red squirrels can be found in the literature.

Natural predators in the case of the red squirrel are birds of prey such as goshawks, owls and pine martins, and they may also be taken by wild cats, feral cats and foxes, in the case of the grey squirrel it is likely

that as well as larger birds of prey they are taken by foxes. David Stock told me of a fox he saw one morning with a squirrel it had partly consumed before caching the remainder under a dry cow pat; another friend Tom, a bee farmer, told me of an incident where he had seen a fox chase and catch a grey squirrel when it dropped down from a bird feeder. It then carried off the squirrel into the nearby woodlands presumably to eat or cache it.

In contrast to the attitudes shown towards the red squirrel in the eighteen and nineteenth centuries there is now great concern over the future of our beautiful native squirrel and there is a positive effort to protect those forests which have a healthy population of reds. Areas of protection in forests where reds are threatened by the spread of the grey squirrel are being established with the purpose of eliminating the greys and providing special food hoppers accessible to the reds but will not allow the heavier grey squirrel to take the food.

Voles (*Cricetidae)*

Voles belong to the family *Cricetidae* and are noted for the fact that their incisor teeth grow throughout life and therefore need to gnaw constantly to prevent them from growing back into the jaw parts.

The Bank Vole (*Myodes glareolus*)

This attractive vole is the smallest of our three mainland voles and as the name suggests is mainly found alongside hedge banks and woodlands as well as in the woods themselves. Voles have blunt noses, small eyes and the ears are flattened close to the body. In the case of the adult bank vole the pelage is a reddish-brown on the upper parts and a silvery-grey on the under parts.

Bank Voles feed mainly on seeds and berries when available but will also eat the stems of woody plants and grass, worms and insects also feature in the diet. In the winter dead leaves are also eaten. Nests consist of chewed grasses and moss, these can be found among the bases of grasses such as cocksfoot, as well in the hollows of tree trunks and the dense vegetation at the bases of hedgerows. In my own garden I often find their nests under corrugated tins put out for grass snakes to bask under. Seeds and berries are often stored as a larder when the weather is unsuitable for foraging. These stored supplies can often be seen when looking for the nests where they can be seen stashed around the outside of the nests.

Breeding

Bank voles in the wild usually start breeding in April and continue until late autumn into December. Captive animals can breed throughout the year presumably because of an assured amount of good quality food and optimum secure and predator-free conditions. Gestation lasts between eighteen and twenty-seven days. The shorter times are for the first-time pregnancies. The number of young in a litter varies according to the habitat but can be up to seven. The young are born naked and blind, at around twelve days the eyes are open and they are weaned between two and three weeks old.

Bank voles are predated on by foxes, stoats, weasels and polecats, and in Scotland pine martens. Barn owls are known to take numbers of young voles. Adders also use their venom to immobilise, track, and then consume them.

The Field Vole (*Microtus agrestis*)

The field vole, or as it often called the short-tailed vole, is probably the most ubiquitous of our native mammals in Britain. In the recent past large numbers of the animals were known to appear in pastures which became known as a plague of voles. Many years ago I remember seeing such a plague in a city location where during daylight hours hundreds of voles could be seen at any time popping their heads up from holes in the grass. The short turf was regularly mown making it easy to spot the animals. These vole plagues were once common in grasslands, but are not in my experience as common as in the past, since I have not seen this phenomenon for many years.

Field voles are brown on the back with a grey underbody and the tail is shorter than that of the bank vole. They are also the bigger of the two species and unlike the bank vole the molar teeth do not develop roots. This vole is found throughout mainland Britain and on some islands but is absent from Ireland.

The diet of the field vole consists mainly of various grasses and green leaves. In dense grasses their runs can be seen by parting the grass, this sometimes reveals little piles of droppings near cropped feeding areas. They are most active at dawn or dusk.

The breeding season is similar to the bank vole running from March to October with a succession of litters of between two and seven young. Gestation lasts around eighteen to twenty days with lactation lasting between fourteen and twenty-eight days.

As well as the usual predators they are also taken by many birds of prey especially barn and tawny owls, and kestrels whose survival is often dependent on the breeding success of this little rodent.

The Water Vole (*Arvicola amphibius*)

The largest of our three mainland voles, and familiar as 'Ratty' in Kenneth Grahame's *Wind in the Willows*. The water vole is one of our most threatened wild animals, once common throughout mainland Britain but absent from Ireland. It has suffered a serious decline according to surveys carried out by the Vincent Wildlife Trust. Numbers are thought to be down by as much as 70% in many areas and up to 97% in Yorkshire. The adult water vole is around the same size as the brown rat and as a consequence is sometimes mistaken for that animal. I once came upon a group of youths on a canal side who were shooting with pistols at water voles in the mistaken belief that they

were rats, after explaining the difference I left hoping that they had taken heed of my explanation.

Since 2008 water voles have been protected under Schedule 5 of the Wildlife and Countryside Act 1981 (as amended). Many Wildlife Trusts have arranged to improve habitats for water voles and have Biodiversity Action Plans (BAPs).

Water voles, as the name suggests, are found along waterways such as slow-flowing rivers and streams as well as canals and ponds, with a good bank-side cover of reeds and marginal water plants. Their runs can be seen leading from a hole and running through the vegetation alongside the waterway, usually there is an area of chewed vegetation around the entrance to the burrow system as well as a small pile of droppings.

The underground tunnel system usually consists of one or more entrances and an underwater exit. Sometimes in clear water, voles can be seen exiting their burrow system below the surface of the water. Nests where the young are born are mainly below ground but, if water levels are high and water permeates the tunnel system, then the voles switch to nesting above ground on a higher level, often in tussock sedges. The diameter of

the entrance holes to the underground tunnel system is about 8cm, around the diameter of the body of a water vole. The tunnel system can be quite extensive with rounded chambers into which nests consisting of finely chewed grasses or reeds are constructed and during the winter months one or more chambers may contain stored food.

Breeding

Breeding takes place from April to September when following a pregnancy of twenty-one days between two and four litters may be born. The litter size is between three and seven young, they are born naked and blind. Growth is fairly rapid with the eyes opening a few days after birth. The youngsters leave the nest when they are around four weeks old and at this stage they appear to be about half the size of the adult vole.

Feeding

Water voles are mainly herbivorous, feeding on reeds and grasses and aquatic plants as well as leaves. When feeding, the vole usually sits on its hind feet holding the grass stem or whatever vegetation it is feeding on in the fore paws and it usually eats the stem rather than the blade. The rest of the plant is then discarded and can be seen lying around the entrances of the tunnel system. When disturbed whilst feeding, a vole will dash into a tunnel and stay just below ground until the possible threat has passed and then will emerge and carry on foraging.

Voles do eat other things as well as vegetable matter, fish are known to be a food item as well as insects and molluscs. According to a BBC report in 2010 it was claimed that in parts of Wiltshire water voles have been recorded eating frogs' legs. It has been suggested that this may be due to a deficiency in the diet of the voles in that area. It was not recorded whether the frogs were dead or alive when taken, I think it would be unlikely that a frog would allow a vole to approach closely without taking avoiding action. Voles need to eat around 80% per cent of their body weight each day and as they rarely appear above ground in the winter months they consequently need to store plenty of food in their tunnel system to survive. This stored food is in the form of grass, reeds, leaves and other vegetable matter, which is taken into the chambers of the underground tunnels.

Mammal predators of water voles consist of mink, stoats, weasels, foxes and domestic cats. Avian predators such as barn and other owls as well as herons will also take voles, as will as large trout and chub.

In the early 1970s in Nottinghamshire voles were plentiful on local canals, streams and ponds. I remember seeing voles at the Attenborough Nature Reserve in good numbers, especially towards dusk when the area became quieter as the public and dog-walkers wended their way home. The Grantham Canal at Hickling was also a stronghold for water voles, they could be seen on almost every visit. Sadly I have not seen them at that location for many years, but I well remember on one visit seeing the nests of the voles dug out on the towpath. I have no idea what animal had done the damage, but since the excavations were fairly neat, it may well have been a mink. Most of the vole holes on the canal side had been interfered with, consequently the voles became scarce at that location.

A few years ago I located a small colony of water voles on the same canal at Owthorpe, they were seen there for a couple of years but sadly seem to have disappeared. At this location I did see and photograph a stoat stalking and successfully taking a family of recently hatched moorhen chicks, so there might have been a connection between the hunting stoat and the absent water voles. The technique of the stoat was to move through the reeds until a chick came close to the bank then the stoat pounced on the chick and with a speed that was almost too quick to observe. It then made off.

In my own village, water voles were present on an old farm pond that became part of a large garden in the heart of the village. The voles were seen regularly by the owner of the property who was extremely proud to have the colony on her land and enjoyed seeing them on her daily walks around the garden. Not far from the site of this colony is the Kingston Brook flowing through the village. In the 1990s I managed to see them whenever I walked alongside the brook. On one occasion I managed to take a photograph of a water vole swimming in the brook. This colony appears to have become locally extinct as I have not seen voles there for several years.

Within the City of Nottingham there is a small brook running parallel to a canal with a footpath between them. On the brook side and close to an industrial estate there was an established colony of water voles which were seen there for several years, feeding on the grass growing on the brook side. Although water voles are said not to stray further than a few metres from the waterside, I have seen at this site a vole on the far side of the canal swimming across the canal towards the brook side where the colony was situated, a distance of at least twenty-five metres. According to a naturalist friend who regularly monitored this vole colony, there have not been any sightings for several years. This coincides with baited traps being set by a pest company a few metres from the waterside where there was a problem with rats near an industrial site. The traps were accessible to the water vole colony. It is to be hoped that voles may not have visited the baited site but have perhaps moved away and may return to this site in the future.

Mice and Rats (*Muridae*)

This family is familiar to everyone, as house and wood mice are known to visit dwellings for foraging opportunities. Many thousands are trapped or killed every year when invading houses. Various kinds of traps are sold for both rats and mice including sticky traps. When the animals are caught by seeking the bait, the fur becomes caught in the sticky substance on the surface of the trap. This type of trap is not humane as the animal can be struggling for a long time before being despatched.

Most of the time mice and rats live outdoors and are of little consequence to man but those that do gain access to our homes can be a nuisance. In my own case I have had my garage invaded by both rats and mice, no doubt attracted by the scent of several bins containing various types of bird seed. In the case of a rat, I was able to persuade my dog to see off the rat but I had to resort to live traps to remove the mice. I have noticed in my captures, that house mice have become rarer over the past few years at least so far as the catches in my garage are concerned.

If I had caught house mice in the traps I could tell what the occupants were by a sweet glycerine type smell near the trap. I remembered the smell from keeping tame mice as pets when a child (pet mice are a cleaned up variety of the house mouse (*Mus musculus*). Wood mice (*Apodemus sylvaticus*), when caught in the live traps, do not give off a strong smell, they do, however, have a strong homing instinct as was shown when I caught a tail-less wood mouse and released it about a hundred metres from the garage. The next day the tail-less mouse was back in one of the traps and was released again at about double the distance from the previous day. The following day the mouse was back in a trap and this time was released at about treble the distance. The mouse found its way back but it took two days to make it back to the garage.

Most rats and mice have tails as long as or longer than the body the exception being the brown or common rat whose tail is slightly shorter than the body. Rats and mice are usually of a brown colour, there are, however, many variations in the coat colour in mammals, such as black or melanistic and white individuals (leucistic) or true albinos which are white-furred but also have pink eyes and noses. My friend Adrian Middleton has written a section on colour coat variations which is included in the book.

The ears of rats and mice are more prominent than those of the voles, the exception being the harvest mouse (*Micromys minutus*) whose ears are closer to the body and this mouse has a more rounded nose than those of the other mouse species.

The Brown Rat *(Rattus norvegicus)*

Probably the most successful mammal on the planet the brown rat, or common rat, has been found on all continents. Originating from central Asia it is believed to have been introduced into Britain in the early 1720s arriving on ships from Russia. The specific name *norvegicus* is a misnomer since its arrival in Norway took place much later than its arrival on mainland Britain, nevertheless, it is some times referred to as the Norway rat. It is also called the sewer rat because of its propensity for exploiting the waste food discarded by humans in our sewage systems. Large populations of brown rats spend their time living and breeding in the sewers and many of them

probably never see daylight except when workers check the sewage systems or descend to deliver poison bait to the rodents.

Rats soon build up an immune system to the various kinds of rodenticides used against them and new ones are constantly being developed. On an agricultural estate I am privileged to have access to, there is a large open barn used to store seed grain before sowing. Rats used to visit the store and take the grain and for some time rats were poisoned by entering covered metal containers containing a lethal rodenticide. Barn owls were sometimes found dead around the estate, and I had one of these birds post-mortemed by a local vet who found the owl had been eating poisoned mice and rats.

The farmland was leased to a shooting syndicate who used to take out the predators such as foxes, stoats and weasels. When the shooting lease was terminated some years ago, the fox population recovered and the problem of rats taking grain ceased. The poison traps became redundant and the rats ceased to visit the grain store for fear of being taken by foxes or owls.

Brown rats are suppressed using a number of control methods. As well as poisons, they are dug out of their holes, trapped, shot and hunted with terriers. Their natural enemies are foxes, stoats, weasels, owls, especially barn owls, while domestic cats and dogs also take numbers of rats. Without this natural predation there would many more rats in Britain as we discard large amounts of human food into the wider environment, mostly in bins that are taken to landfill sites. It could be said with some truth that the success of the rat depends on humans for its greater survival in the wild.

The diet of the brown rat consists of anything that is edible to humans but there is a preference in rural areas for grain such as wheat and barley as well as root crops. Animals are taken live or as carrion. I well remember catching mice in an open trap in my garage. One evening when I entered the garage to check the catch, a rat jumped out of the trap. It had been eating the mice caught in the trap. Having lived in a rural situation for more than fifty years we notice that after harvesting has taken place the rats are displaced from the arable fields and come into the village, we then see rats around the compost bins and in the hedgerow, we leave it to the foxes to clear out the rats which they usually manage to do within a few days.

When we first moved into our village around forty years ago the back garden backs onto open countryside consisted of a few ancient apple trees and a row of Brussels sprouts, the rest being grass. In the corner of the garden there was a large compost heap that was well compacted. This soon became a home to a family of rats, as was indicated by a number of tunnels into the heap and little pathways leading from the tunnels into the garden. The tunnels are around 6 – 9cm in diameter. The old apple trees were mainly miniature ones and carried a few different varieties of apples, some sweet, some less sweet. I began to notice that the rats were taking the apples from the ground and into the tunnels of the nest site. The rats carried the apples in their teeth holding the apple above the ground, invariably choosing apples of a size that would fit the entrances of the tunnels. I removed the apples from the ground and the rats then climbed the trees taking the sweetest apples and removed them to the nest site, always taking apples of a size that would fit the entrances. Continuing the experiment I removed all the apples from the sweetest tree and the rats then took the less sweet apples until all the small trees were stripped of apples. This left a large tree carrying cooking apples, which although appearing less palatable, were being taken from the tree. All the apples were then removed from this tree by hand, leaving the rats to take the windfall fruits wedged on the top of the hedge.

The apple experiment I think shows the widely recognised intelligence of rats. Rats make extremely good pets as was shown when we bought a white rat for our son. This rat lived in an open cage in our son's bedroom, free to come and go as it pleased. The pet rat would leave its cage and wander the bedroom and visit its owner whilst in bed and never once did the rat make a mess other than in his cage.

Brown rats are capable of delivering up to five litters of young a year, with an average number of young between seven and eight, the gestation period is twenty-one days and they are weaned at around three weeks of age and capable of breeding from eleven weeks old.

The Black or Ship Rat (*Rattus rattus*)

The black rat now probably one of the rarest mammals in Britain, was introduced during Roman times in the first century AD and was said to be responsible for the Bubonic plague spread by fleas. Although it is commonly referred to as the black rat, not all the rats are black, some populations are of a brownish colour with grey bellies, others are brown with a creamy belly. They are smaller than the brown rat with a longer tail, whiskers and ears. More partial to living indoors and well adapted to climbing trees, in parts of Asia they are said to build their nests in trees. The diet is similar to the brown rat although the black rat is said to prefer fruit when available. The reproductive cycle of the black rat is similar to that of the brown rat with a gestation period of twenty-one days and with a similar number of litters.

Because of its propensity for living in buildings and the control measures carried out in such places against rodents, the black rat may have had its distribution reduced by the use of rodenticides and the destruction of warehouses and dockyard buildings where they were commonly found. It is now reported to exist in only one or two places in mainland Britain, London and Avonmouth and in the Channel Islands. It is also reported to occur in a few Scottish Islands.

Another cause of the decline of the black rat may have been the extraordinary success of the brown rat, it probably took over much of the habitat of its smaller cousin when extending its spread over the whole of Britain.

In spite of public hatred of rats in general, in parts of Asia they are regarded as sacred animals and are fed in some of the temples where they exist in their hundreds. They can of course spread diseases, the main one being leptospirosis. In Britain miners were said to be at risk since they often fed rats and mice whilst eating their sandwiches underground. The pit rat population was sustained not only by eating the sandwiches fed directly or when discarded but also by taking food which was stored underground to feed the pit ponies when they were a common source of haulage.

The Wood Mouse (*Apodemus sylvaticus*)

This ubiquitous mouse is found throughout Britain and is able to exploit every kind of habitat except purely aquatic ones and the higher mountain regions. It is a native mouse, largely nocturnal with protruding eyes, large ears and a tail that is as long as the head and body together. The underparts are greyish-white and the body is of a yellowy-brown colour although, as with most mammals, the colouration is variable and some animals are of a melanistic kind with completely black fur.

The mice live in a tunnel system where they store food and produce their young. When active above ground, wood mice move around with quick jerky movements and jump when alarmed or disturbed.

Like all mouse species the incisor teeth grow throughout the life of the animal. Wood mice are able to exploit a wide variety of different kinds of food from animal to vegetable but they feed mainly on seeds and, when in season, fruits, nuts and berries. They also consume the larvae of beetles and other invertebrates including earthworms.

Breeding takes place from early spring to the autumn when litters of between four and seven young are born naked and blind. The eyes open at around twelve to sixteen days and they are weaned at around eighteen to twenty-two days from birth. The lifespan of the wood mouse in captivity is probably as long as two years, in the wild the lifespan is greatly reduced from a few weeks up to a few months.

They can be a problem when entering buildings such as grain stores and barns. The farm cat is often seen stalking around the farm buildings and is employed to try to control the numbers of mice taking the precious grain. Rodenticides are also used against the mice although they can often affect the natural predators such as owls and foxes through a build-up of the poisons found in the contaminated carcasses of the deceased or dying mice.

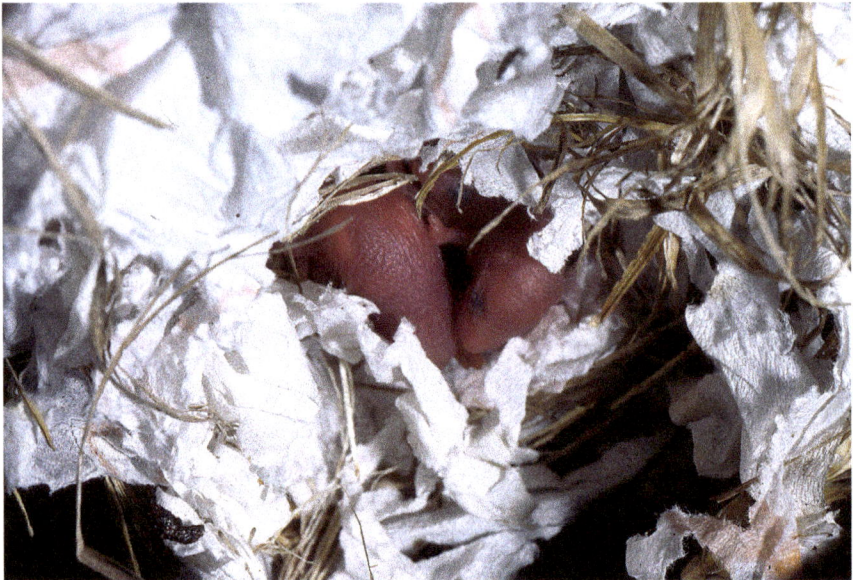

The Yellow-Necked Mouse (*Apodemus flavicollis*)

This mouse has all the characteristics of the wood mouse but is the larger of the two species and has a distinctive yellow band on the neck and the base of the tail is thicker than that of the wood mouse. This mouse when handled can be very vocal and will bite more readily than the wood mouse when being removed from traps.

The yellow-necked mouse has a more restricted distribution than its close relative, being found mainly in the south and south east of England and the Welsh borders. I have only encountered this mouse once, that was in Woodchester Park in Gloucestershire whilst attending a course there many years ago. Feeding is rather similar to the wood mouse but the yellow-neck is more inclined to climb in search of food.

Breeding is said to be a few weeks earlier than the wood mouse and produces bigger litters with up to eleven young. Its gestation period is similar to that of wood mice as is development and weaning.

Harvest Mouse (*Micromys minutus*)

The harvest mouse is the smallest rodent in Britain; this attractive little mouse was first reported as a separate species in 1767 by Gilbert White of Selborne. Around the same time that White noted the difference between wood mice and harvest mice, the German scientist Peter Pallas on a collecting trip to Siberia in 1768 collected harvest mice and reported the first description of the animal he had taken from the banks of the River Volga. Pallas is therefore credited with the actual scientific discovery of the harvest mouse (Stephen Harris, *Secret Life of the Harvest Mouse*).

Harvest mice were once found in cornfields, building their nests within the fields of grain which in White's days were safe from the sprays of modern agricultural farming which drench the fields with herbicides, pesticides and fertilisers several times during the growing period.

Rodents are not the only animals to succumb to the drenching sprays, leverets are known to perish by being chilled from the spraying operations

as well as being squashed by the heavy machinery. Harvest mice used to perish when straw burning was legal. Thankfully this threat is now removed and straw is now used for fodder and bedding for farm animals, it is also being used as fuel for large central heating units.

The fur of the harvest mouse is a light sandy colour on the upper surface with a pure white belly, the ears are small and carried close to the body, the eyes are black, protruberant and rather like a smaller version of the wood mouse eye. Young animals when weaned are a brownish colour rather like the house mouse and achieve the typical adult colour within a few weeks of leaving the nest. The first and second digits of the hind feet are opposable enabling the mouse to grasp stems, the tail is prehensile and acts as a fifth limb assisting with balance and supporting the mouse by wrapping around vegetation when climbing.

The harvest mouse is the only rodent to build aerial nests, these are usually built around two-thirds of the way up the stems of grasses and reeds. They are woven from the living plant material making them flexible, thus enabling the mouse to push its way into the nest without

leaving an entrance hole visible. These aerial nests are used for breeding during the summer months as well as for resting in, they last well into autumn and winter and are useful for checking for the presence of harvest mice when doing survey work. Sometimes nests are built near ground level often in the heart of tussocky grass such as cocksfoot and other coarse grasses.

Ground nests are mainly used during the breeding season when the weather is inclement and wet for long periods, heavy winds can also

play havoc with aerial nests forcing the mice to build their nests at a lower level.

The breeding season starts in late May and extends through to early autumn, after mating there is a gestation period of around eighteen days. In captivity up to eight litters can be born with up to seven young in a litter. In the wild fewer litters are born, perhaps as few as three in a season.

Harvest mice feed on a wide variety of seeds from cereals and wild plants, insects and their larvae are also taken often in preference to seeds. Over many years I bred harvest mice in captivity and fed them on a mixture of wild bird food containing millet, carrot seeds and wheat. Wild fruits such as blackberries, hips and haws were also fed as well as insects, such as flour beetles, their larvae (mealworms) and blow-fly (bluebottles) and their larvae.

In Britain wild harvest mice are found mainly in the south east of the country but records show the animals to be present south of Edinburgh. These are isolated small populations and because of their isolation can be considered vulnerable. One of the first local records for harvest mice I obtained in 1965 was from an animal caught at Wiverton in south Nottinghamshire. A friend, Malcolm Walker, was exploring an area where a local gamekeeper was walking along the road pushing his bicycle when they stopped to chat. Whilst they were conversing a mouse ran across the road. The keeper pushed his front bike wheel in front of the mouse and picked it up and showing it to my friend explained that it was a harvest mouse. Soon after that I went to the area and searched the coarse grass verges and found several aerial nests and I then checked the banks of the River Smite nearby and located several more nests.

Harvest mice are predated on by all kinds of animals including foxes, stoats and weasels as well as domestic cats. Avian predators include owls especially barn owls. Young mice are often taken as they are especially vulnerable because of their lack of experience outside the nest situation.

The House Mouse (*Mus domesticus*)

The house mouse is a non-native species that most people have seen either in their house, garage or outhouse. This mouse is widespread in the British Isles and Ireland and is of a greyish-browny colour with a tail that is thicker than that of other mice and scalier. House mice were probably introduced into Britain as long ago as the Iron Age and are known to travel on ships. It has been reported that the mice that live on refrigerated vessels grew longer hair as a result of the cold conditions.

The house mouse is dependent on man for its existence and does not thrive well in outdoor conditions. When the residents of the Isle of St Kilda abandoned the island in 1930 the house mice, which were numerous on the island and dependent on the islanders for their existence, became extinct.

Breeding takes place throughout the year with a gestation period of between nineteen and twenty days when litters of between five to eight young are born naked and blind and are weaned at about two weeks of age. Once the young have left the nest their survival depends upon the habitat. Those living an outdoor life have a much shorter lifespan than their cousins living in a sheltered indoor life who may survive up to two years. House mice are predated upon by most small carnivores. Rats are also known to kill them.

Dormice (*Gliridae*)

Two members of this family are present in mainland Britain, the common dormouse also known as the hazel dormouse (*Muscardinus avellenarius*) which is our native species, and the fat dormouse (*Glis glis*) or edible dormouse which is an introduced animal with a limited distribution. Once kept by the Romans in clay pots known as *gliraria*, the fat dormouse was fattened as a food animal. *Glis glis* was introduced into Britain by Walter (later Lord) Rothschild into his private collection of animals at Tring in Hertfordshire. The resultant spread of the animal into the Chiltern Hills where they are common is said to have been the result of escapees from this collection.

The Common Dormouse (*Muscardinus avellenarius*)

Sometimes called the hazel dormouse the common dormouse is one of our most threatened mammals. Largely a southern species there have been a number of attempts to spread the animals by introductions to areas which may have had the animal in the past and where it has not been seen or recorded for many years or centuries. In Nottinghamshire there was a single record of the mouse in the Victorian County History at Arnold in Nottinghamshire, and since no other records appeared the mouse was believed to be extinct. Re-introductions were made in several counties including Derbyshire, and Nottinghamshire, where it was introduced to an ancient woodland in the north of the county. Although the mouse is believed to still survive there, it is disappointing that it was not thriving.

There may be more hope that the mouse will eventually succeed in becoming established since there have been more animals introduced to some of the original chosen sites in more recent years.

The common dormouse, like its introduced relative, hibernates for up to six months of the year starting in October. Although it may rouse for short periods during hibernation it is unlikely to leave the nest unless it becomes flooded or damaged in some way. By hibernating when its natural food is scarce or not present, the dormouse can survive longer than small rodents which must keep feeding throughout the year thus using up much energy. The life span of a wood mouse is but a few months whereas the dormouse can live up to five years in the wild and longer in captivity.

Dormice can, in inclement weather during the summer months, enter into a torpor whereby they are able to lower the body temperature thus saving energy when food supplies are limited or scarce. Dormice are easy to handle during the torpid state as they are slow to warm up and consequently are vulnerable at this stage. I have seen the mice in this state whilst checking dormouse boxes in a Staffordshire wood with the Staffordshire Mammal Group. Several dormice were seen during the foray as well as wood mice and common shrews. One of the dormouse boxes checked contained a female together with several young mice. On opening the box the mother ran up a tree whilst the young were weighed and checked over before being put back into the box to await their mother's return, which I was assured would be within a short space of time.

Common dormice feed on a wide variety of tree flowers and fruit, and thrive better in more ancient woodland where there are more species of trees and shrubs. Such woodlands usually have a rich understory of bramble and hazel, these supply flowers and fruit but also enable the mice to climb through the tangle of vegetation to access the fruits of the trees, ash and hawthorn being particularly important. Nuts are chewed in a characteristic way, this enables the presence of dormice to be detected. When opening hazelnuts the dormouse holds the nut in its forepaws and rotates it whilst chewing, leaving a smooth round opening with fine chisel type indentations on the outside of the chewed hole. Insects are also taken, possibly in the form of aphids, and it is likely that caterpillars of many species of moths and butterflies are also eaten.

Breeding takes place when the animals are fully active after awakening from hibernation, possibly in June and carrying on into summer through to autumn. Litters can consist of up to eight young but smaller litters of around four or five young are more usual. The gestation period is between twenty-two and twenty-four days, the young are born naked and blind in nests woven from shredded honeysuckle or dried grasses. The nests are situated sometimes near ground level in dense vegetation or in natural tree-holes often metres from the ground.

Where dormice are being monitored, nest boxes are placed on trees with an entrance hole facing the tree trunk. The boxes are designed to open easily in order for the mice to be checked. Nest boxes are probably helping dormice to maintain or increase their numbers, especially in areas where natural nest sites are lacking.

The future for the common dormouse is perhaps as good as can be expected with a greater awareness of their requirements. Captive breeding programmes and subsequent releases help restore or maintain their numbers by introductions or re-introductions to areas able to sustain viable populations of the animals. The linking of dormice habitats by providing a corridor whereby the animals can expand their range will help ensure that existing populations of dormice can spread to new sites. Rope ladders stretched across busy roadways enable the mice to expand their range by being able to take advantage of the safe crossings and spread to other

suitable sites without the consequences of risking crossing roads at ground level.

Owls take dormice but in fewer numbers than other small rodents, weasels as well as foxes and other carnivores also take the mice. Most casualties probably occur during hibernation when the mice are unable to take evasive action. Those animals with low fat reserves are most likely to succumb, especially during long cold winters.

The common dormouse is strongly protected by law. Under Schedule 5 of the Wildlife and Countryside Act 1981 (amended 1988) and by appendix III of the Berne Convention, licences are required to handle or disturb the animals.

The Fat Dormouse (*Glis glis*)

The fat dormouse is found naturally throughout south – western Europe and was introduced into Britain in 1902 to Tring Park in Hertfordshire, the home of Walter Rothschild who later became Lord Rothschild. Having once been introduced, some of the animals escaped and spread into the Chiltern Hills where the species thrives. Although it has not spread so rapidly as the introduced grey squirrel, it may in future times increase its range.

The fat dormouse is rather like a small version of the grey squirrel although the squirrel does not hibernate, and the fat dormouse hibernates from October to May. Captive fat dormice often do not normally hibernate, especially if kept in sheltered conditions enabling them to continue to feed throughout the

winter months. In these conditions they can survive for more than ten years but wild living animals may have a shorter lifespan.

Fat dormice are protected under the 1979 Berne Convention on the Conservation of European Wildlife and Natural Habitats as signed by the United Kingdom, and under the Wildlife and Countryside Act 1981 the animal cannot be captured without a licence and once captured it cannot be released back into the wild.

Feeding consists of all kinds of fruits, nuts and insects and carrion is also eaten. They are particularly fond of apples and can be a nuisance with stored fruit in the autumn. As well as eating stored fruit they can be a nuisance by chewing electricity cables and making nests in attics and roof spaces.

Sometimes the mice hibernate together, possibly in family or social groups. Nests are of a domed shape and are usually constructed in shrubs and dense bramble and honeysuckle patches, and are made of shredded honeysuckle with leaves and grass incorporated. The mice are social animals and several mice may share the same nest. They may also hibernate below ground where they have occasionally been discovered when excavations are taking place. When such discoveries are made several mice have been found hibernating together. Fat dormice will also enter roof spaces to hibernate, often a number of animals may be found wintering together. Hibernation for the fat dormouse can take up to seven months or longer which means the mice have to store large quantities of fat under the skin to survive the hibernation period.

Breeding takes place in August or September and it is likely that only one litter consisting of up to eleven young are born, but a more usual number would be between four and six. The young are blind when born, the eyes opening between twenty-one and twenty-three days, the young leaving the nest at around a month old.

Predators of dormice are tawny owls, mammal predators include stoats and weasels as well as domestic cats.

Over many years I kept fat dormice in secure housing, once in a garage and second in a specially adapted shed with an outdoor run. The mice bred in captivity when kept by a naturalist friend. He obtained the mice from a captive population, from a study trial in the south of England. I and another naturalist were given a pair each on the understanding that they could never be released and must be securely caged. My original pair lived more than ten years with the freedom of a garage in which to exercise and sleeping quarters in a cage near to the roof of the garage. Whenever I wished to tempt the dormice into their sleeping quarters I would place half an apple into a large net and hold it near a mouse. It would then climb into the net and when this was held near the cage it would climb into the cage.

The dormice never hibernated whilst in captivity except once. When checking for the mice I noticed that one of the mice was not around the cage and I searched the garage and found the missing dormouse behind a bench curled up on the concrete floor and for the first time in ten years it was hibernating. I decided to leave the mouse in its dormant state on the floor.

Sadly a few days later on checking the dormice, I noticed that the hibernating mouse was still on the ground and was breathing very slowly but there was a large wound to the base of the skull. It appeared that a rat had gnawed through the wooden rear door of the garage and attacked the hibernating mouse. Bringing in my dog eliminated the rat but sadly because of the extent of injury to the skull of the hibernator, I had to humanely destroy the dormouse.

Because of my success in rearing the first pair of dormice, after their death I was offered a second pair of animals. These were from the same original population and were related (brother and sister). This pair were given special secure accommodation with a pen on the outside of a shed, a nesting box was attached to the inside of the shed with two entrances each leading into a separate sleeping area. The mice would on occasions sleep together in one section of the box, on other days they would choose to sleep in separate sections. They were fed in the external pen where they drank from a drip bottle and took their food on a ledge. None of the dormice I kept ever bred or so far as I know attempted to mate. This pair also died in their tenth year. One day I had noticed that both mice were becoming weak and were eating less but still continued to drink regularly, one of the dormice died shortly after taking a drink one morning, and within a few hours the second dormouse was dead. I often wonder if the second to die was influenced by the death of the first animal, not a scientific hypothesis but such incidents are often reported in the human population.

Rabbits and Hares (*Lagomorpha*)

In Britain we have but three members of the order belonging to the family *leporidae*. The mountain hare or blue hare is largely confined to the Highlands of Scotland and, in a slightly different form in Ireland it is known as the Irish hare. Introductions have been made to several islands in Scotland as well as into the Peak District of Derbyshire and South Yorkshire. These more southerly introductions were made for sporting purposes around the 1880s. The brown hare is the largest of our three lagomorphs and is well distributed throughout Britain. Rabbits are familiar to everyone and are found throughout the British Isles and the island of Ireland. They form part of Beatrix Potter's stories as well as in literature generally and they are of course in a cleaned up form kept as pets by children, and also by rabbit fanciers who exhibit them in shows.

The Mountain Hare (*Lepus timidus*)

The mountain hare also referred to as the blue hare is a true native of the British Isles and Ireland and has been introduced to several Scottish Islands. It is found more commonly on the eastern side than on the west side of Scotland. The mountain hare turns white, or with some individuals partially white, during the winter months. Moulting takes place three times during the year achieving the white pelage in time for the snowy season. Mountain hares are said to turn white earlier the further north they are located.

The mountain hares introduced into the Peak District of Derbyshire during the 1800s turn white in varying degrees, some completely white whilst others show varying degrees of whiteness.

Mountain hares are distinguished from brown hares by their smaller size, having shorter black-tipped ears. The upper-side of the tail is white, outside the winter season the pelage is lighter than that of the brown hare or rabbit. Like the other members of the lagomorph order the mountain hare has a secondary set of upper incisor teeth behind the large chisel-shaped first incisor teeth. The teeth are rootless and grow throughout life. Another feature of this order is a process known as refection whereby after feeding a soft pellet is produced and eaten, later the familiar hard pellets are voided, most of the food having passed through the gut twice. Mountain hares are usually found in upland areas of Scotland and the areas where they have been introduced. The Peak District population is found on higher ground than brown hares although the two species are known to have occurred in the same habitat and there are records of interbreeding between them. Feeding consists of varying types of herbage, in Scotland heather is the most important food source. Creating heather suitable for maximising numbers of red grouse for shooting purposes, is achieved by burning off the older growths, thus encouraging young shoots to appear, this also suits the hares as tender shoots of heather (*Calluna vulgaris*) are preferred. Cotton grass (*Eriophorum spp*) as well as other grass species are also eaten, as well as various shrubs. The bark and leaves of several types of trees are also taken according to seasonal availability.

Mountain hares breed in the early part of the year from February in the Peak District and about a month later in the Scottish population. The hares gather in small groups during daylight hours when courtship takes place. After a gestation period of around fifty days, litters of one to four young are born. The young are born fully furred and with the eyes open and are weaned around four weeks later. Three litters may be born in a year. Sometimes severe weather can cause a high mortality rate in the earlier litters and those born later in the year are also vulnerable. Hares can live up to nine years and possibly even longer. Captive animals freed from the hazards of wild living may like other captive species achieve a longer survival rate.

All lagomorphs, including mountain hares, are predated on by foxes and stoats, and in Scotland wildcats will take both adults and leverets. Golden eagles as well as buzzards and other large raptors will take leverets. Shooting by man is probably the main factor in the mortality of hares, especially in Scotland.

Viewing mountain hares usually requires some scaling of high ground and a good pair of binoculars although they can sometimes be seen at close quarters when out walking in the high ground in the Peak District or in the Highlands of Scotland. I have watched mountain hares whilst walking the Derwent Moors in Derbyshire along with my late friend Len Needham, where sometimes one can almost tread on a hare before it breaks cover and races ahead. From the car park at Long Gutter Edge near Glossop I have watched hares in the winter on the slopes above the disused railway line. After a careful scanning with binoculars, small white shapes could be seen among the boulders. The hares are in forms (lying-up places) consisting of chewed-off stems of heather into which the hares can press their bodies to provide some concealment from predators. They also dig out simple burrows up to two metres long in the peat and can sit in the entrance partly concealed. Towards evening the white shapes begin to emerge from the shallow forms and burrow entrances and start to move around on the slopes. The hares are beginning to set off on their nightly foraging.

Brown Hares (*Lepus europaeus*)

Brown Hares are the more familiar of our two species of hare, being more widespread than the mountain hare and the largest of the lagomorphs. Because of their less demanding habitat requirements and its more adaptable feeding strategy, brown hares rely on lowland farmland usually below 150 metres. Introductions have been made into Ireland and into some counties for hare-coursing purposes but they do not thrive like the mountain hare and are therefore less common.

Brown hares are thought to have been introduced to Britain during Roman times, they are accepted as a fascinating animal in the British landscape. They are found wherever there is a farmed landscape producing a variety of cereal crops, along with some grassland and wooded areas.

Feeding on various grasses and on the earlier stages of growth of cereal crops, hares seem to prefer the younger fresh shoots for their forage rather than the coarser stages of later growth. Wild grasses are preferred to the commercial crops and in the summer months many herbs are eaten. In wintry conditions and sometimes in the summer, hares can be seen in woodlands where they browse on various trees and shrubs.

During daylight hours, hares lie up in shallow scrapes on cultivated land or depressions in grass fields, these scrapes conceal the animals throughout the daytime making the animals almost invisible to human eyes. In the evening, they begin to stir and sit up, when they become conspicuous and are then able to be spotted. Whilst watching badgers in woodland I have frequently seen hares move silently through the woods occasionally browsing on their way and on occasions crossing the badger sett itself.

Breeding

Usually breeding takes place in the springtime which accounts for the so called mad March hares, when several males can be seen chasing a female coming into season. There is certainly a lot of activity at this time including the boxing sessions when the females can be seen turning whilst being pursued by one or several males and standing on their hind legs and fending off the ardent males by striking with their forelegs, males respond by striking back in a similar fashion.

After mating there is a gestation period of between forty-one and forty-two days and up to four young are born, although in my experience litters of between two and three leverets seem the norm. Leverets are born fully furred with their eyes open. Born together the leverets soon move to their own

forms, consisting of longer grasses and are usually fairly close to each other. Leverets are suckled for a few minutes once every twenty-four hours usually in the evenings. When first born, leverets weigh only around 100g and are weaned at around three weeks old or later.

In parkland where I had permission to study the wildlife, I watched a female hare during the daytime hanging around a particular area and assumed she had leverets somewhere in the area. A friend David who was working in the same piece of parkland also observed the hare loitering in the same place during the daylight hours and did a search of the coarse grasses on the perimeter of a mown area and found a single leveret crouching in its form well concealed, and matching the coarse grasses perfectly. We decided that we would return later that day and watch for the female returning to feed her young. It was springtime when at around 11pm it was completely dark, we watched with binoculars and saw the female hare move towards the leveret discovered earlier. When she got near the spot where the leveret was lying, two leverets emerged and went up to the female and began suckling, the mother sat upright and within a few minutes the young had been fed. The mother then moved away and the youngsters began to roam around on the grassland and we followed them at a distance and took some photographs. The surprising thing was that the leverets seemed to move through the grasses creeping along like hedgehogs rather than the short jerky movements of their cousins the rabbits.

Whilst taking field classes in Leicestershire on one of the Wildlife Trust reserves we sometimes found leverets concealed in the long grasses, usually after a quick look we would cover the young animals with vegetation and leave them hopefully to cope with their survival strategy. At this stage the leverets are thought to be scentless and as long as they remain still are often overlooked by predators.

One February morning whilst driving along a village road with a friend, Peter Shakespeare, we noticed a pair of crows diving down onto the snowy fields and what appeared to be a small animal jumping up towards the crows. I immediately stopped the car and we climbed the gate to the field to get a better view of what was taking place. As we approached the scene we could clearly see that the animal in question was indeed a small leveret that was bravely defending itself, jumping up as the crows dived down, it was rapidly rotating its forelegs in a circular motion in trying to defend itself.

The crows which no doubt might have taken out the eyes of the leveret had we not intervened, soon moved away.

As I had my camera with me I knelt in the snow and prepared to photograph the lucky animal. Kneeling down I edged forward closer to take the photograph, and began focussing the camera when to my complete surprise the little leveret leapt towards me rotating its forelegs and uttering a low grunting sound, I was not prepared for the attack and fell backwards into the snow. The little leveret weighing no more than a few grams had startled a human weighing many kilograms causing him to overbalance and crash to the ground. My friend found the incident highly amusing as I did later. Before leaving the scene we steered the leveret towards a dense hedgerow concealing it with some dry grasses, hoping the crows would not now be able to detect the young animal again.

In January, a few weeks before the above incident, I was told of a visitor to a small rural hospital who whilst walking along the drive bordered by a well-stocked shrubbery, noticed a small leveret tucked into its form in the grassy edging between the road and the planted area. Most leverets are born during the early spring months and on into the summer months as indicated by the courting of hares in March which leads to the well known mating behaviour pattern of 'Mad March Hares' as described above. The above examples show that a number of young are born during the winter months in spite of the spring and summer mating rituals. Individual hares can often be seen running frantically across the fields and appear to be following a scent trail as they twist and turn, this apparently random behaviour is I believe a male hare following the scent of a female coming into season and the male is able to detect her by following her scent trail. I have observed this type of activity throughout the spring and summer months.

Where there are good numbers of hares and little disturbance from shooting or illegal coursing activities, the hares can become quite tame and will tolerate being stalked with a camera. I well remember stalking a well-grown leveret having spotted it for a number of days in the same place. Approaching the hare whilst it was basking caused it to move slowly away, and following it, I kept well back until the hare settled down. Then creeping forward until I was standing directly above the animal, which made no attempt to move away, but began to shake nervously, at which point I decided to back away slowly and leave the animal to its own devices. The hare had perhaps thought I was a predator and had become mesmerised and was waiting for an attack that may have eliminated it.

Adult hares can become accustomed to the proximity of humans and through regularly seeing them can become quite accepting of their regular appearances. One particular animal, which I am sure got to know my vehicle, would approach the car whenever I drove into the area and would come up to where I was parked and settle down nearby. This hare would begin grooming itself or simply close its eyes for a while crossing its forelegs and take a short nap. I was able to get some very close-up shots of the animal when it was so engaged. This particular hare had a distinctive mark on its head just above the eyes and so was easily recognizable.

Another example of the acceptance of human presence by hares was brought home to me whilst holidaying near Malham in Yorkshire. I went to watch a badger sett on a gill-side and became absorbed by the behaviour of the badgers when they started digging rather noisily sending boulders clattering down into the water. As I was sitting with my back against a stone wall, I became aware of a hare lolloping towards me along a well-worn badger path. I had previously noticed a rectangular hole in the wall just to the right of where I was sitting. To my astonishment the hare approached me, we were both at eye level, and after a short hesitation when it first sensed me, the hare then passed through the hole in the wall into the field beyond.

I could easily have touched the animal as it passed me by.

The next two nights when I went to watch the badgers, exactly the same routine happened and I was able to watch the hare scale the gill, then following the badger path towards where I was sitting. It then went through the hole in the wall. Making every effort not to disturb this trusting animal, I concluded that this was a female hare that may have had leverets nearby, and was making her nightly visits to suckle them.

Rabbits (*Oryctolagus cuniculus*)

Rabbits are familiar to us all especially as they feature regularly in literature for children through the writings of Beatrix Potter and others, especially the tales of Peter Rabbit which most youngsters have met with at home or in school.

Many of us have kept rabbits in a domesticated form and there are many breeds from the giant rabbit, so called Belgian hare, to some of the smaller breeds such as the Dutch rabbit. Rabbits reproduce well in captivity and enthusiastic keepers of the animal compete with their pets in special shows held throughout the country.

The wild rabbit is common throughout Britain and was once thought to have been introduced by the Normans, but after remains of a butchered rabbit dated at around 2000 years old were dug out on an archaeological dig in the village of Lynford in Norfolk in 1905, it looks as though the rabbit may have been introduced by the Romans. It is possible rabbits were brought over as food animals. Originating from Southern France, Iberia and North Africa, it is thought the rabbit has been transported to every continent except Antarctica.

The Normans established rabbits in enclosures known as warrens, which were surrounded by walls. Inevitably some animals escaped and set up their warrens in hedgerows and other sheltered areas. Rabbits were introduced on to some offshore islands, where they survived and thrived due to the lack of predators. They are still commonly present on a number of islands including the well-known islands of Lundy and Skomer.

The deadly viral disease *myxomatosis* came in to Britain in 1953, many people believed the disease was introduced deliberately. The disease spread rapidly through the rabbit population and it was estimated reduced it by 99%, thus creating problems for predators such as foxes, which had to hunt more frequently for smaller species such as field voles. The rabbit population has partially recovered and it is estimated that there are now around half the number of animals as there were before the outbreak of disease.

The disease persists in the rabbit population and outbreaks are still seen from time, though these are sporadic and localised and have nothing like the drastic effect of the original infection. Over the last few years I have had to despatch a number of animals with the disease, which might have been spread by the rabbit flea. Some ten years ago we regularly saw up to eleven rabbits in the field at the back of our house, but after an outbreak of the disease the numbers are down to less than half and recovery seems to be taking a long time.

Feeding

Rabbits feed on a variety of grasses, and shrubs such as furze but can be a great nuisance to farmers by eating cereal crops such as wheat and maize, especially when these are in the early stages of growth. During the winter months when grass growth slows down, rabbits turn to eating the bark of trees, this can cause serious damage in woodlands. Newly planted saplings have to be protected by tree guards to minimize rabbit damage.

Like other lagomorphs, rabbits produce soft faecal droppings, these are produced in the caecum after grazing and are eaten when resting, usually underground. This is known as refection, this enables the animal to pass the food twice through the alimentary canal. In adverse weather, rabbits can stay underground by consuming the soft droppings thus avoiding the need to emerge above ground. A second pellet in a hard form is voided and these are the familiar droppings which are also used as territorial markers, and can often be seen on high ground and on tree stumps.

A more favourable view of the rabbit can be considered, on nature reserves, often on chalk grasslands where rare plants such as orchids are found, the grazing produces a short sward benefiting native wild flowers. For this purpose rabbits are fenced in to create conditions benefiting the flora. After the 1953 *myxomatosis* epidemic there was a drastic effect on the flora of the chalk grasslands, the consequent loss of wild flower habitat resulted in the areas becoming scrubland, where once orchids had flourished.

Living communally in a warren enables the animals to maintain a safe haven in times of predation or other disturbance. When disturbed each animal would know where to bolt to obtain a safe haven. In a large warren there may a number of dominant bucks and does, each pair taking over the more favourable parts of the underground system. The young or non-breeding animals would make do with the areas not taken over by the dominant animals.

Not all rabbits live communally in warrens. When young I along with friends used to borrow a neighbour's dog, which from memory was an Alsatian-type animal, we would take the dog onto an area of rough grassland which had a number of gorse bushes scattered sporadically throughout the area. There were no warrens on this rough piece of land and the rabbits used to live and breed within the dense clumps of gorse. The dog would circle one of these gorse clumps barking furiously until a rabbit broke loose, whereupon the dog would chase and invariably catch the fleeing rabbit. Then rabbit was a common food animal and we enjoyed a number of delicious stews made from the catch.

Another example of rabbits breeding above ground is in my present garden where I have left an area wild, together with a pond and a log pile attracting a number of wild animals including great crested newts and grass snakes. Within the log pile over the years, rabbits have produced several litters of young. There is not enough room within the stack of logs for more than a few animals and the young soon move away when they are a few weeks old. The rabbits originate from a friend's orchard nearby where there is a small warren consisting of a few holes. The low number of rabbits suggests that the local fox population holds down the numbers with their nightly visits.

Rabbits have a number of ways of communicating with each other. Communal areas of droppings indicate the demarcation of territory or the extent of the warren and can be marked by large numbers of droppings in a particular area. Both does and bucks have glands situated in the anus which indicate the sexual status of the animal when linked to the droppings. Urine is also used as means of communication. Rabbits also have a scent gland situated under the chin used as a means of communication, this is carried out by the rabbit rubbing its chin along the ground or on a twig leaving a drop of scent indicating its sexual or social status. A dominant buck or doe would be able to let lower status animals or competitors know of its presence by these indicators.

So far as vocalisations are concerned rabbits are limited as to the sounds they produce. A low grunting sound is made when domestic rabbits are handled. When attacked by some predators including dogs, or wounded, they are capable of emitting a loud squealing sound. (I have heard hares give off a similar squeal when they are wounded during a shoot).

Thumping the hind legs hard on the ground is often used as a warning by hares and rabbits when they are alarmed by the presence of a predator near the form or warren. The thumping warns other members of the group of possible danger. This signal may also warn other animals of possible danger, for example rabbits living near to a badger sett or perhaps living in part of the sett would transfer the sounds by vibrations to the badgers who would then be ultra cautious before emerging.

Breeding

The breeding season of rabbits can last from January through to August. Does usually dig out a single blind hole known as a stop and line this with fur from her belly, mixed with dry grasses to make a nest. After a gestation period of around thirty days the doe gives birth to litters of young which number between three and seven. The young are born naked, blind and deaf, and are suckled once a day usually in the evening. When the doe leaves

the stop she seals the entrance with soil or other debris. Stops can also be situated within part of the main warren. When the young are around ten days old the eyes open and youngsters appear above ground at around three weeks of age, they are weaned a few days later.

Predators of the rabbit include most of our native carnivores, they are taken by foxes and badgers who can locate young rabbits underground by scent. Badgers dig straight down into a stop and take them, foxes usually open up the stop and dig their way down to the young rabbits. At a later stage when the youngsters are above ground they are available as a food source to a greater number of carnivores, such as stoats, weasels and polecats, and in Scotland, the wildcat. Feral and domestic cats take both adult and young rabbits. I remember a neighbour's cat used to visit a field opposite our house on a daily basis and return home carrying an adult rabbit, sometimes the prey was a full-grown animal. Rabbits are also taken by birds of prey such as the golden eagle, red kites, goshawks and buzzards. Owls also take the young rabbits as do some of the smaller raptors.

Because of their breeding success and mainly underground secure habitat, rabbits remain one of the most successful animals in the British countryside and in spite of damage caused to agricultural crops remain a popular sight for many on their trips to the countryside.

Deer (*Artiodactyla*)

There are six species of deer living in the wild in Britain, all belonging to the family *Cervidae*. Of these only two are thought to be native, the red deer and the dainty roe deer. The other four species have been introduced. The reindeer (*Rangifer tarandus)* is present in the Cairngorms in Scotland but is not living truly wild as they are subject to a management regime and as such really are farmed animals. Reindeer were once present as a native species but it is thought they became extinct before Roman times.

Red Deer (*Cervus elaphus*)

The largest of our native land mammals and probably the most magnificent and imposing of all our British wildlife species, red deer are found all over the British Isles and are present on many islands as well as the mainland. Scotland has the largest population of deer. Shooting estates fence in the animals to preserve the best heads as trophy deer. There are thought to be around 300,000 red deer in Scotland. In England red deer are present in many forests, Thetford Chase in Norfolk is a stronghold and there are remnants of an ancient population in Sherwood Forest in Nottinghamshire. Many estates and country parks have herds of red deer in semi-wild conditions, there is a fine herd at Bradgate Park in Leicestershire the former home of the ill-fated Lady Jane Grey. Here the deer have a section of the parkland kept free from visitors, and enjoy an area of oak forest which closely resembles their native habitat.

Red deer are really forest animals but because we have fewer forest areas than some other European countries the deer roam the open hills

and moorland especially in Scotland. The deer attract naturalists and other visitors who wish to see and photograph these inspiring animals. Another attraction is the sporting side where stalking and the shooting of a specimen stag with a fine set of antlers is the aim. Many sporting estates fence in their animals to ensure the best stags are retained for stalking. I was told by one stalker in Scotland that the estate had even imported stags from one of the deer parks in southern England because of their superior heads, sporting large antlers, and therefore of attraction to foreign visitors who are said to pay up to a £1,000 for a trophy animal.

A red deer stag stands at the shoulder between 100 – 135cm and weighs around 190kg as a mature animal, whereas the females known as hinds are rather smaller at around 100 – 120cm at the shoulder and weigh on average 120kg. Red deer like all deer are ruminants, feeding voraciously on herbage, mainly choice grasses such as bents and fescues then resting whilst chewing the cud. Whilst they are lying down chewing the cud, there are usually one or two animals that are alert looking out for possible predators. Most ruminants use this behaviour pattern as they are mainly herding animals and need to find a safe place to digest their food.

Breeding

Mating known as rutting takes place in the autumn months from mid-September through to November. Mature stags gather the females, known as hinds, into harems where they constantly chase and attempt to keep together, until they are in season and ready for mating. During the rut there is much roaring from the stags, apparently the loudness of the roars attracts the hinds. The stags having the loudest calls are likely to attract the most hinds and are therefore likely to sire the most calves. The dominant stags do not have it all their own way and are constantly challenged by less dominant animals resulting in much fighting, using their antlers as a trial of strength. During these battles there are often injuries and there are records of fatalities from sustained injuries and on rare occasions both animals may die from their wounds, especially when their antlers may become locked together.

By the time the rutting season is over the stags are completely worn out as they rarely feed during the rut. They then spend most of their time feeding-up and preparing for the shedding of their antlers and getting ready

for the new season's growth. Antlers are shed from March to April, the budding new antlers start to develop shortly after the old ones are shed and when growing have a blood supply, which is carried in a soft growth surrounding the developing antler. This covering is known as velvet. Stags in velvet find the new growth rather sensitive and are careful to avoid catching their heads against hard objects such as a tree branch. The growth of the new antlers is a rapid process and by the end of July they are fully developed.

The young of the red deer are known as calves, and are born after a gestation period of eight months. When born the calves are hidden in a bracken patch or some other form of cover and are suckled by their mothers, weaning takes place at around eight months. Single calves are born to the hinds, although rarely twins are known to occur.

Outside the breeding season stags and hinds separate and form herds of animals of a similar age structure and sex, although hinds often have calves with them. There is little conflict between stags or hinds outside the breeding season thus giving time for the stags to feed up and save their energy for the forthcoming rut.

Feeding

Deer are browsing animals taking the best food available according to season, in the spring and summer months when the grasses are growing these are then chosen, they also browse on sedges and rushes. Feeding in winter consists of evergreens like ivy, the shoots of trees are also eaten as well as the bark. Ferns are eaten, as is heather and for those animals that have access to them various seaweeds are also part of the diet. The many deer in parklands have their natural food supplemented by the feeding of corn and root crops such as kale and beans, since natural feeding is limited by the size of the park, and areas used for games and other entertainments.

Because deer have no natural predators now that brown bears and wolves are extinct in Britain, their numbers have to be contained by shooting. Hundreds of deer are taken each year by this method. In the New Forest for example of six species of deer are taken out by expert marksmen employed by the Forestry Commission. High seats are used by the marksmen and these are placed in some of the deer's favourite haunts, thus the marksmen are able to select weak and injured animals first, before selecting other animals to achieve a balanced figure of each species for the forest to support. Without these culls the tree damage would become serious and deer would need to wander from the forest to find suitable browsing thus becoming endangered by having to cross roads in search of forage.

The other of means of control would have been by hunting with hounds, which used to be practised but is now illegal. When legal this method accounted for only a few deer as it was an entertainment rather than a control method. Shooting by stalking is a method carried out as a sport which accounts for a number of deer especially in Scotland, where the aim as mentioned earlier is to shoot deer with a large set of antlers as a trophy. The Red Deer Commission For Scotland manages a control system catering for all the species of deer in the country. Deer as a wild animal are not owned by anyone, landowners are expected to control the numbers on their land. Some deer are fenced in to provide a guaranteed number of stags for sporting purposes. This fencing can create problems for other species such as the much-threatened capercaillie, which when flying has a tendency to crash into fencing, often with disastrous consequences.

Fallow Deer *(Dama dama)*

Probably the most attractive of our six species of deer and the one that has the most variable coat colour variations. Fallow deer are the species that we are most likely to see in the numerous deer parks scattered around the country. In my home county of Nottinghamshire and in the neighbouring county Leicestershire there are plenty of fallow deer. Wollaton Park in Nottinghamshire and Bradgate Park in Leicestershire and many deer parks throughout Britain have herds of fallow deer. The deer in these parks are mostly of a spotted variety known as common, a variety that retains its white spots in winter, the menil. The other colour varieties of the animals are the dark and the leucistic or white deer and the *melanistic* that is a black or dark-coloured animal. White deer are popular in some parks, these deer are not albinos, they do not have pink eyes. The white colouration is retained by the removal of any deer that are not of the favoured colour, thus preventing them breeding with the preferred white variety.

Herds of fallow deer are found in the wild in many woods and forests throughout Britain. In Nottinghamshire they are found in Clipstone Forest and in Annesley Park. The deer living in wild conditions are usually of the dark or leucistic variety. During the rutting season the bucks roam widely hoping to locate does that are in season. I have seen bucks crossing the busy A614 road, dodging the traffic and causing motorists to take evasive action to avoid contact. Collisions with a deer can cause considerable damage to a vehicle as well as the deer, which may be killed or require veterinary treatment.

Fallow bucks when mature have *palmated* or flattened antlers, these are evident from the age of three years, they also show a prominent Adam's apple. Some bucks when fully mature carry a magnificent head of antlers, fine specimens of which can be seen in Boulder Wood in the New Forest.

Breeding

During the rut which runs from late September and peaks around mid-October the bucks can be heard making their groaning calls and dashing around to keep the does together on their rutting patch. They also use up much energy chasing other young bucks away who come in and try to take some of the does away from the herd. Whilst rutting, bucks of equal status carry out a ritualised parallel walk. When the two bucks walk side-by-side occasionally stopping to spar, then carrying on walking before returning to the does.

After mating the bucks come together again and concentrate on feeding and restoring the huge amounts of energy lost during the rut. The does, meanwhile, will feed up in preparation for producing the fawns which are born between late May and mid-June. The fawns will be weaned by October. Young bucks will stay with their dam until they are around eighteen months of age when they will join the buck herds.

Feeding

Fallow deer feed very much like red deer, grazing on grasses and reeds during the favoured spring and summer months and browsing trees and

other foliage throughout the year, especially during the autumn and winter months. Because of a limited supply of natural feed in deer parks during the winter months, supplementary feeding is required.

Having no natural predators, fallow deer like all the other species of deer in Britain are controlled by shooting, this is undertaken by skilled marksmen in the case of the state-managed forests. All species of deer are enjoying a boom in numbers and sadly this often leads to conflict in the case of damage to farm crops when some deer are shot with inappropriate weapons, sometimes leading to animals being wounded and suffering a lingering death. As mentioned earlier, large numbers of deer are involved in collisions with motor vehicles with inevitable consequences both for the deer and the unfortunate motorist. Some authorities are trying to reduce the numbers of accidents involving deer by persuading the deer to use underpasses, and to cross busy roads using bridges specially made with the sides concealed with vegetation. This avoids the nervous animals having sight of the endless stream of traffic on the roads below. Many years ago when the M1 motorway was being constructed through Nottinghamshire herds of fallow deer near the Annesley estate were encouraged to use an underpass under the motorway to access their traditional feeding grounds on both sides of the new road. The deer eventually accepted the underpass. For several years after the motorway was opened, deer still tried to cross the busy M1 and were found injured or dead after creating an enormous amount of chaos. Dr Donald Chapman (co-author with his wife of the book *Fallow Deer,* published by Terence Dalton (1975)) wrote to me asking for information concerning the deer crossing at Annesley, asking if the deer were using the crossing. He was working on deer crossing motorways and other busy roadways. After examining the slots (hoof prints), these were evident in the mud. I was able to inform him that deer were indeed using the crossing.

Fallow deer are, along with red deer, the two species of deer most people would recognise when visiting deer parks where they are usually kept in fairly large numbers. Both species are herding animals and are therefore easy to locate, they also become relatively tame by seeing people on a daily basis. Deer bring interest to parklands and allow many city dwellers to experience contact with some of our largest wild animals not easily seen in the open countryside.

Roe Deer (*Capreolus capreolus*)

The roe deer is a truly native species which became extinct in England in the eighteenth century. It was thought to have survived in woodlands in the Highlands of Scotland. Roe deer were thought to have been introduced into southern England around 1800 and others introduced into East Anglia in the late 1800s. Roe deer are now spreading throughout the Midlands and have been seen in Nottinghamshire over the last twenty years or so since the 1990s. In south Nottinghamshire, the deer have been seen in several parishes including the one in which I live. In July, 2013, a roe buck passed alongside our house attempting to access a grass field at the rear, but was thwarted in its attempt when our neighbour, riding his motorbike, suddenly appeared. The startled deer then came out of the entrance to the field and made off towards the village centre. This was during the rut when no doubt the buck was seeking a mate, and had wandered away from the woodland area where I have sometimes seen them. Both my wife and myself have over years seen roe deer crossing the roads near the village during daylight hours. I have also been able to take photographs of a buck in early October on private land in the village.

Roe are not herding deer like the red and fallow, they are usually seen in small family groups consisting of a buck, doe and a pair of kids. The most roe I have seen locally was a family group of five animals. In another location within the city boundary in a cemetery I have seen a winter herd of seven roe which consisted of two bucks, two does and three well-grown kids.

Roe deer do not usually show in fields or woodland edges when there are cows, sheep or other farm stock, preferring their own kind to associate with. In an area of private farmland surrounded by woodland I am privileged to access, I regularly saw roe deer particularly during the weekends when farming activities ceased, however, when a local dog owner was given permission to walk his hound on the land, the roe deer ceased to visit the walled former parkland. He was walking the dog around the perimeter of the land and I believe the scent from the dog, which would be easily detected by the sensitive nose of the deer, caused the animals to stay away from this otherwise ideal habitat.

Feeding

The food of roe deer is similar to the other species, being both a grazing and browsing animal. It feeds mainly by browsing hedgerows eating buds and shoots. Bramble is important and the deer I have observed also feed by grazing on grasses in between the browsing sessions.

Breeding

The rut takes place from mid-July to the end of August and can cause bucks to wander across roads in search of does on heat. After fertilization, females undergo a period of delayed implantation rather like the badger and are the only deer to undergo this procedure. Through delayed implantation, the blastocyst does not implant in the wall of the uterus until late December or early January when the embryo starts its development and kids are born mid-May to mid-June. Usually twins are born but triplets are not uncommon. The young are suckled shortly after birth and are left alone usually in a patch of bracken or coarse vegetation, and if twins or triplets are separated. This is presumably to protect individual fawns from predators, who may find one but not necessarily all the animals.

Roe deer are easily recognised when the face is visible as there appears to be a moustache effect where a black band running from the nose to below the lower jaw, no other deer exhibit this facial feature.

Vocalisations consist of short barks given out by the does when alarmed or disturbed, also from bucks during the rut. Does emit a high-pitched squeal especially when they are in season. In between these commonly heard calls there are variety of other forms of calling.

Bucks rub their antlers against young trees when marking territories and can cause some damage to young plantations, this fraying results in the rubbing off of bark sometimes completely ringing the tree. Where roe deer have been courting, a ring consisting of a worn circular path of bare earth where the buck has been pursuing the doe round and round a small tree, usually a birch tree, is plainly evident.

It has been estimated that there are around 500,000 roe deer in Britain so the future for the roe deer looks secure. Though not as easily observed as the herding deer such as the red and fallow, this attractive deer can be seen on the edges of woodlands and sometimes in arable fields especially in the early mornings and at dusk.

Roe deer are moving into urban situations in some large cities such as Glasgow, and can be seen there in the cemetery, they can also be seen in a new cemetery within the city boundary of Nottingham as mentioned earlier. This can only be seen as a welcome addition to the flora and fauna of these relatively quiet and peaceful locations.

Sika Deer (*Cervus nippon*)

Sika deer are a native of East Asia, they have been introduced to many countries in Europe, including Britain and Ireland, and have also been introduced into New Zealand as well as South Africa and America. The introductions into Britain threaten the gene pool of the indigenous red deer where the sika can interbreed with the red deer. Herds of sika deer in Ireland are also known to threaten the genetic integrity of the native red deer population. I have seen both species in close herds in Ireland in the hills of Killarney. Here they are controlled to reduce the risk of hybridisation with the red deer.

Sika are a woodland deer and are associated with the woodland edges where they can browse on the various shrubs and bramble layer, and graze on the grasses, sedges and seeds such as acorns. Sika deer are active throughout the twenty-four hours unless disturbed by man when they can become more nocturnal.

they are weaned at around four-months-old. The young stags then move out and the hind calves tend to stay around longer with their mothers.

Sika deer are smaller than red deer and are probably one of the most successful species for survival rates. In the New Forest in Hampshire around a hundred sika deer are culled each year and are kept apart from the red deer to avoid hybridisation.

Although most sika deer have spotted coats in the summer months and darker coats in the winter months, in the Purbecks in Dorset, white sika deer have been seen and photographed in the area. These colour variations have been noted for a number of years and although not true albinos make an interesting addition to the normal – coloured animals.

Muntjac Deer (*Muntiacus reevesi*)

The muntjac deer, also commonly known as the barking deer, was introduced into Woburn Park in Bedfordshire in the early twentieth century and soon spread as escapees and releases into neighbouring counties. They are often seen in Leicestershire where I have photographed them, I have also seen them in Nottinghamshire whilst carrying out survey work relating to badgers.

This small deer is seen in well shrubbed woodlands where they tend to skulk in the undergrowth appearing initally as rather humpbacked when retreating into cover. The males are known as bucks and the females as does, the young are referred to as fawns. The face of the muntjac deer is

quite unmistakable from any other species having a rather narrow face with dark markings which run from the nose to the small antlers in the males.

A feature of this deer is its loud barking call when calling to the opposite sex or as a warning call when disturbed. Once whilst looking for the purple emperor butterfly in Fermyn Woods in Northamptonshire, I came across a buck that followed me through the woods as I walked along a ride. The deer walked parallel alongside me as I made my way through the woods walking along a ride, it kept just inside the woodland barking continuously for the whole time I remained in that part of the wood, and only ceased the barking when I turned off the ride and walked in the opposite direction.

Breeding

Muntjac deer do not have a traditional rut as the other species of deer in Britain do, but breed all the year round, this no doubt accounts for their success, and puts them in a bad light as far as forestry is concerned. Like roe deer they fray young trees but at a lower level, often such barked trees either die or are deformed and as such become unsuitable for commercial forestry purposes. Muntjac deer can breed from five to seven-months-old, and there is a gestation period of 210 days from conception to birth. The young are weaned at around seventeen weeks. They can live for a long time and in captivity have been recorded up to nineteen years for a female and sixteen years for male animals.

This small deer is a browser rather than a grazer, feeding on brambles, leaves, ivy, nuts and fruits. Grasses are taken especially in springtime when leaves and fruits are scarce or absent.

Chinese Water Deer (*Hydropotes inermis*)

A native of China, this small deer was introduced into Britain and kept as an exhibit in London Zoo in 1873. After some thirty years some animals were transferred to Whipsnade Zoo. Other animals were transferred to collections and parks and they were first reported in the wild in the early 1940s. The animals are now well established in the wild in the eastern counties of Norfolk, Suffolk, Bedfordshire and Cambridgeshire.

As the name suggests this deer is found in the areas of fens and water habitats, where the reed beds and woodlands suggest its native homeland. Although this deer is capable of strong swimming it can be found in areas of a drier habitat such as that in Whipsnade where it occupies areas of open grassland bounded by woodlands.

Chinese water deer are between the size of the roe deer and the muntjac deer and are unique in that the males do not grow antlers but have large upper canine teeth protruding well below the lower jaw. The large canines are used for defence and attack during the rut, during their tussles the males can sustain injuries from the canines. These tussles are carried out by the males carrying the head below the body thus bringing the canines in line for the best position for striking a blow against an opponent.

Breeding

Rutting in Britain occurs in December, the gestation period is reckoned at around 165 – 210 days, the young are born from May to July and are left in secluded places, the doe returning to suckle them several times a day. The fawns are usually left singly, but occasionally twins or more are found together. Chinese water deer usually have more young than the other species of deer in Britain. Although they are a more productive species they seem to be slow to spread, the reason for this is believed to be a high mortality rate during the winter months.

The calls of the deer consist of barks when alarmed which are heard more frequently during the summer months. When chasing one another a whickering sound is made. During the rut whilst pursuing females the males emit a squeaking or whistling sound.

Chinese water deer seem to have found a niche in Britain and cause little damage compared with other species, their food seems to consist of mainly browsing on various types of vegetation, herbs, weeds and grasses. They will also nibble the tops of root crops such as carrots and winter wheat on arable land, but not to great economic significance.

It has been suggested that there are more Chinese water deer in Britain than in their homeland of China and Korea. This deer seems to have found a niche for itself on the east coast of England and provides an interesting addition to our fauna, long may it thrive!

Cattle (*Bos taurus*)

The semi-wild cattle of Chillingham Park in Northumberland are well known. They have been enclosed for some 700 years and consequently are inbred, the genetic strain is said to benefit from the fact that the bulls fight for dominance and consequently the fittest and strongest bulls are the ones that mate. The animals are much smaller than commercial breeds and are very selective as far as feeding is concerned. The Chillingham cattle are said to only eat untainted grass or hay. During the severe winter of 1947 they were in severe danger from extinction as the animals refused to eat cattle cake or oats. Their numbers dropped from the forties to thirteen animals, consisting of five bulls and eight cows. Clearly some action had to be taken to ensure that if this herd died out then another group of animals would have to be established to ensure the survival of these rare animals.

Consequently in 1970 a herd was established in northern Scotland. The present status of the animals at Chillingham is heartening, as the herd total in December 2013 was 101 animals.

Bats (*Chiroptera*)

The order *Chiroptera* is represented by two families in the British Isles, the horseshoe bats *rhinolophidae*, consisting of two species, and the rest are the *vespertilionidae.* Horseshoe bats are so called because of the horseshoe shape on the nose also known as the noseleaf. *Chiroptera* literally means 'hand-winged'. All bats have four fingers between which is stretched the wing-membrane, the thumb is a small limb attached to the wrist and when on the ground together with a short foot assists the bat to walk and sometimes literally run. Bats are the only mammals that are capable of true sustained flight, animals such as the so-called flying squirrel are merely gliding using the loose skin attached to the legs, this is stretched to enable the animal to glide from tree to tree.

The horseshoe bats lack a tragus in the ears, present in all the *vespertilionid* species. The tragus is an extra lobe arising from the base of the ear helping to redirect the returning calls when the bats are hunting their prey. Prey are located by echolocation, the calls made by the bats through the open mouth are bounced off the prey and picked up by the bats as echoes returning to the ears. The tragus helps direct the returning echoes into the ears of the *vespertilionid* bats, and is of a different shape for each species, this also helps with the identification of species. Echolocation also assists the bats in finding their way around their habitat, which they are able to do with remarkable efficiency.

In the case of the horseshoe bats the calls are made through the nose-leaf that helps in directing the emitted sounds, the returning echoes are picked up by the ears, as in the other species.

The calls from each bat species have their own frequency, which may differ between feeding and when socialising. These high-frequency calls are made audible to human ears with bat detectors which lower the frequency of the calls and enable them to be identified as the various separate species.

There are generally reckoned to be sixteen species breeding in Great Britain, with a possible seventeenth, the greater mouse-eared bat. This bat was last recorded as a single animal in Kent in 2006. In previous years this bat had been recorded in Dorset, West Sussex and Kent. Since the records of this species are fragmented and usually consist of a single specimen, the bat could easily be extinct in these counties.

Bats are long-lived animals and there are records of bats exceeding twenty-five years of age, small species such as pipistrelles can live up to eleven years. It has been suggested that the maximum age for any of the *vespertilionid* species is thirty-three years (Macdonald, *Encyclopedia of Mammals*). The average survival age of the British bat species is, however, much lower than the maximum ages quoted.

Feeding

All the British species are insect feeders, the type of insects eaten vary between the different species. Generally the smaller species take insects such as gnats and midges, whilst the larger ones take beetles such as cockchafers and dung beetles. Long-eared bats prefer moths when available. I have often located the feeding places of brown long-eared bats by looking for the wings of moths which are discarded on the ground below a feeding perch, sometimes in a house-porch.

Bats often take their prey on or near the ground, when they can be caught by cats, sometimes they evade the cats but suffer damage to the wing-membrane causing them to have impaired flight or worse be unable to fly at all.

I have kept several species of bat that have suffered from damaged wing-membrane, and depending on the amount of damage they can sometimes regrow the membrane. When healed, bats can be released back into their environment but this should always be in the area where they were first located.

In the case of bats unable to be released they can help with education, children and adults are able to see and study the animals at close-quarters.

This can help bats as there are many rumours, mostly false, such as bats getting caught in the hair when flying close to humans. Bats do fly around the heads of people on warm summer evenings, the reason for this is that people often attract midges and gnats, and the bats are simply trying to catch these as food.

Breeding

Bats are slow breeders, producing only a single young from the age of two or three years, weaning takes place at around forty-five days when the young begin taking insect food for themselves. When born, the young are naked and blind and totally dependent upon their mother. Their growth and food intake is dictated by environmental factors such as the temperature in the nursery roost and the external temperature dictates the volume of insects on the wing. Bats must conserve their energy and will avoid hunting where the prey is scarce.

Hibernation

All the British species of bats enter a period of hibernation during the winter months, this means that when food is scarce or absent, bats are able to conserve their energy by staying within the roost. When roosting, bats mainly get into crevices in brickwork or often between window frames and in hollow trees. Horseshoe bats are the ones often pictured hanging head down, from walls or the roofs of caves, with their wing membranes wrapped around the body. Hibernation sites must be humid or the animals could become dehydrated. A constant temperature is also a requirement, generally caves where hibernating bats are found have a stable temperature and a constant humidity. Bats do occasionally stir during the hibernation phase, it is thought that the need to urinate causes this rousing. When roused the bats may fly when seeking prey that may be available at the time. I have seen a noctule bat flying during the winter in a park within the city of Nottingham, this was a fine sunny day and it is possible that there may have been some suitable prey items on the wing.

Whilst licensed to handle and photograph bats, I visited many roosts and once on a routine visit to a roost in Thrumpton, Nottinghamshire, I was shown some bats living in the attic space of a house. Children played in the attic and the owner had divided up the space to allow the bats to be undisturbed whilst the children were playing there. The bats were *Leisler's* and were breeding there. I was delighted to have been shown the roost and identified the animals, the owner had thought they were the more common *Pipistrelles.* The bats used to exit the attic by following the cased piping into the kitchen and left the house by an open window. Sadly several years after I had first visited the roost there had been some soffit boards replaced and the access point for the bats had been blocked off preventing the animals from accessing the roof space.

An interesting incident took place when the vicar living in the vicarage opposite our house called me to look at a bat hanging in the porch. I identified the animal as a young *pipistrelle* and brought it home to check out. I fed the bat some mealworms and the next night I took the bat outside intending to place it on the wall so that it could take to the air. Opening my hand I was amazed when an adult bat took the young bat from my hand and flew away with it. The young bat had evidently been calling out and the mother had recognised her voice and collected it before I could place it on the wall. This clearly shows the echolocation abilities of both adult and juvenile bats.

Bats of all species are threatened by a shortage of prey species and

a reduction in suitable roosting places. Agricultural sprays such as insecticides must have an impact on the insects available, also some treatments for cattle have an impact on the larvae which feed on the cowpats and affect the development of dung beetles which are an important item in the diet of some of the larger bat species. Timber treatments for wood-feeding insects have in the past affected bats, as the animals used to get the insecticide onto their fur and when attempting to lick this off would ingest it proving fatal to the animals. Two churches in the village where I live appear to have lost their bat populations, the parish church had the timbers treated shortly after we came to live in the village some forty years ago. Bats were seen in some numbers every evening during the summer months, before the treatment took place. The Baptist church became disused, I saw brown long-eared bats in the building before it become redundant. The church eventually became a dwelling, and although provision was made for the bats to access the building the colony seems to have disappeared. The fact that nowadays one sees very few insects killed by colliding with cars, while thirty years ago cars would be covered in the remains of insects such as midges or moths, which shows how the insect population has been affected.

We now only see two or three bats during the summer, these are *pipistrelles,* our commonest bat, whereas at one time we saw and heard

through the bat-detector a number of species, including whiskered bats (*Myotis mystacinus*). I once found a whiskered bat dead on my drive one morning and was able to take it into school and show it to the children. Schoolchildren seem to delight in seeing dead specimens of any sort, and, with proper precautions, in handling them.

Greater public awareness of the plight of bats and an awareness that they are not offensive but fascinating animals to be admired should help to ensure their future but we need to tackle the causes of their decline.

Bats are well protected under the Wildlife and Countryside Act of 1981 and other legislation, but the problem lies with our treatment of the greater environment and the use of chemical insecticides which devastate the insect population and consequently the bat's future.

Seals (*Pinnepedia)*

We have two species of seal around our coasts, which belong the family *Phocidae,* the common or harbour seal, *Phoca vitulina,* and the grey seal, *Halichoerus grypus.* Both species feed on aquatic animals, mainly fish, of many species according to what is seasonly available. As well as fish they also take cephalopods such as squid and octopus.

The grey seal was among the first mammals to be protected under the Grey Seals Protection Act of 1914, today seals are protected by the Conservation of Seals Act of 1970. Eating fish brings seals into conflict with man and there is a close season for shooting them which runs from the 1st of September to 31st of December, that is when seals are breeding. Although seals can be shot at any time if there is damage to fish stocks or nets, in case of a serious outbreak of disease or other factors which threatens the seal population shooting can then be banned.

The common seal in spite of its name is the less common of our two species, and is the smaller animal. Common seals have rounded heads with v-shaped nostrils and long whiskers, the ears being covered by fur are not visible. The grey seal has a long nose, and the nostrils have vertical slits, it is also much larger than the common seal.

Breeding

The males of both species are known as bulls whilst the females are called cows, young seals are known as pups. Common seals mate in July and are pregnant between ten and eleven months which includes a period of delayed implantation. A single pup is born in June – July often in a sandy cove and after feeding on the mother's rich milk is weaned after two or three weeks.

The female then comes into season and is mated. Grey seals have a different breeding pattern from the common seals, pups are born on land between September and December according to location. The population of grey seals at Donna Nook on the Lincolnshire coast for example produce their pups around November – December, whilst those on the south west coast are born about a month earlier. Like common seals, the pups are weaned after two to three weeks.

Most populations of grey seals are found around the Scottish coasts, only 10% are found around the English coastal areas. The fierce weather during the winter of 2013 separated many grey seal pups from their mothers and one rescue centre in Norfolk had taken in over a hundred pups into their care. Those pups when weaned would lack the experience of dealing with extreme weather and become disorientated, and unless taken into care would most likely perish. The pups are cared for, and when their fat reserves are restored and they have moulted from their white coat and have developed their first proper coats, they are released back into the area where they were first located.

Young seals have large brown eyes making them appealing to humans and probably contributes towards their survival when taken into care, since they attract financial contributions.

Disturbance by walkers especially dog walkers, and at sea, damage from

boat propellers cause injuries, sometimes fatal. Disease is also a threat to seals. Other threats to seal populations come mainly from man especially as they are dependent on fish species some of which are favoured by the human population.

Both species of seal found around the coasts of the British Isles are monitored by the Sea Mammal Research Unit (SMRU). They are based at the University of St Andrews, Fife, Scotland. This scientific body reports to government and advises scientists on the status of the seal populations.

COLOUR VARIATIONS

Adrian Middleton

Introduction

Sunlight is the source of much of the colour seen in nature and the bright colours of the rainbow tell us something about its components, but not everything. The reds, yellows, greens and blues, and the others which we see, consist of a narrow range of wavelengths within the whole spectrum. There are many other wavelengths, including infrared and ultraviolet light, which are normally invisible.

The various forms of pigments are in fact simply colouring agents which may also take on other roles. These include the biological pigments which absorb certain wavelengths of light and reflect those remaining, so producing a particular colour. Most do this but one form of the pigment melanin is unusual in that it can absorb all light so what is seen is plain black which is not really a colour at all. As a separate concept to pigments, the effects of structure can also produce colours from light whether by a process of reflection or iridescence. The colours seen in the wings of a butterfly for example are the result of both biological pigment and structural influences on light. These and related phenomena will be mentioned again in the following pages.

Differences in colour and colour patterns help in part to differentiate between many of the creatures which we see, especially those which are closely related. Sometimes colours serve other purposes. The bright eye-like markings on the wings of some of our moths and butterflies may deter a hungry bird or the black and white stripes on the badger's head may warn others of its powerful bite. In contrast the white rump patch of a roe deer bounding away could make other deer take heed of approaching danger. Brightly coloured feathers and striking markings can be used to impress a potential mate whilst the finely patterned brown and buff feathers which closely resemble leaves and twigs provide perfect camouflage for the nightjar and woodcock when resting on the ground, helping them avoid detection.

As darkness falls, however, sight largely loses out to scent, sound and touch. Special adaptations can then come into play. For example, many bats specialise in the use of echolocation during darkness to find their prey and some night-flying moths take advantage of ultraviolet light to locate the flowers that provide them with nectar and pollen. Sometimes there is no sunlight at all and to compensate for this a number of deep-sea creatures, as well as some familiar terrestrial insects such as glow-worms, have evolved to produce light in various colour forms by using chemical reactions in their bodies.

The tapetum, a light-reflecting layer in the retina of the eyes of mammals, facilitates vision in fading light and is well developed in those that are nocturnal. The glaring eye, sometimes seen in reflected torchlight, can also be found on photographs taken with flash, something of an aggravation to many photographers!

The retina of the eye contains rods, responsible for determining light intensity and cones, responsible for colour. The behaviour of the badger in the way it appears to dislike strong light, but can discern objects in poor light, suggests that its eye contains high numbers of rods but few cones. This animal also appears less able to see red light, which supports these observations too. Like many mammals, badgers are considered to be colour blind and it is only in the higher mammals such as the primates, along with birds and others, that colour continues to play a significant role. How some of these actually see colour remains something of an enigma.

Colour Formations

How colour is produced depends on the characteristics of the animal under consideration and so on the mechanisms available to create it.

Many colours stem from the amounts and type of the pigment melanin which is produced in special cells (melanocytes) mainly in the deeper layers of the skin of the animal, bird or other creature. From there melanin also reaches hair, nails, hoof and horn and also feathers and scales. Parts of the eye (including the iris), inner ear and areas of the brain also have some melanin.

Melanin comes in two forms: eumelanin, which is responsible for the black and brown colours, and pheomelanin, which is responsible for the reds and yellows. The absence of one or other, or both, of these types of melanin are relevant in the cases for example of albino and erythristic badgers, which are discussed later. Both these types of melanin are also often present together but in different quantities, so this can affect the final colour.

Melanin is generally important but particularly in mammals, which rely on its effect almost entirely to produce the colour of their fur and skin etc. Even in the mandrill, the well-known African primate, it is melanin interacting with light that is responsible for its spectacular blue facial and rump markings, where there is no fur, rather than any other pigment type. Similarly the blue eyes of the young fox cub are the consequence of effects of light in the presence of only a small amount of melanin. As the fox cub grows the amount of melanin increases and so the eyes turn brown. Exceptionally though, pink colouration, for example in the eyes, may be due to the colour of the blood pigment haemoglobin when the effects of melanin are missing. The question of the colour green also arises. In the sloth of South America, the green colour is due to green algae on the fur.

However, other pigments can be involved. In birds, as well as the effects of melanin, some plumage colours show when light is refracted in the complicated structure of the feathers resulting in blues and reds and some other colours. One such example is the kingfisher showing the iridescent green and blue plumage on its back, as it flies downstream and out of sight. There are also pigments such as carotenoids. When flamingos feed on various invertebrates including brine shrimps containing carotenoids, their feathers turn from white to pink.

In cold-blooded animals including reptiles, amphibians, fish, squids and octopuses, special cells (chromatophores), are also the sources of pigments. These cells are responsible for producing skin and eye colour and can lead to a wide variety of pigment including black, yellow, blue, red and iridescent.

Amphibians provide an interesting example of how different colours can be created. Not all are produced by pigments alone, for example the greens and blues are produced by the refraction of light. In the frog, which has a thin translucent skin, light is able to penetrate into the layers of melanin where some wavelengths are absorbed. Some are not and these are then changed by the iridescent cells into the colour blue. The blue changes to green when it interacts with the yellow pigment in cells near the skin surface. Also, the changes in the skin from lighter to darker appearance are due to the movement of pigment in and between the cells. Temperature and moisture levels also contribute to these changes (M. Smith).

Butterflies and moths, taken as examples of insects, have scales on their wings and bodies which are the source of their colours and their arrangement forms the pattern and design of their markings (M Brooks & C Knight). Pigments, whether derivatives of uric acid or melanin, are responsible for most of the colours in the scales. Those derived from uric acid include the white in the white butterflies and yellow in the yellow butterflies such as brimstones and clouded yellows. Most of the blues and metallic shades are of structural origin. Such colours are produced by the ridged structure of the scale itself which breaks up the light that falls on it causing changes in the colour and intensity according to the angle from which the wing is viewed, as in the case of the purple in the male purple emperor butterfly or the green in the green hairstreak butterfly (Ford). The eyed hawk-moth exposes the brightly coloured 'eyes' on its underwings when disturbed - an example of 'flash colouration'.

The glow-worm, one of our most unusual insects, is in fact a beetle. The male is fairly typical but the female is not. She has three pairs of light-producing organs containing luciferin (light-bringer) backed by a reflect of minute crystals carried under her abdominal segments. The pale-green light produced by oxidation of the luciferin glows in the dark and so attracts male beetles to her.

The Moult

Moulting usually applies to the shedding of fur or feathers with subsequent regrowth.

Two moults per annum are normal for our mammals, one in spring and one in autumn. All the carnivorous mammals and some others in Britain have an outer coat comprising guard hairs with the softer undercoat of finer and thicker hair which is usually less obvious.

The coats of deer can be quite a different colour after the spring or autumn moult. The roe deer often has a much redder appearance in summer and is greyer in winter. Sika deer and fallow deer show rather similar variations.

Some mammals can change colour dramatically over a very short period of time. The stoat is usually rich reddish-brown throughout most of its range and for most of the time. However, in the far north, such as in the Highlands of Scotland, it turns white in the late autumn, sometimes over a matter of only a few days, although retaining its black tail tip. Before the autumn moult, the next coat of hair, in this case white, is already growing and it quickly becomes apparent when the old summer coat is shed, so helping camouflage the animal in the winter snows. These colour changes depend on the winter climate, taking changes in the natural daylight and air temperatures into consideration. The spring moult in stoats is little affected by climate and the new coat is brown. The mountain hare also turns white rather similarly in winter. In this case, the colour change relates to the light, not the temperature and the spring reversal may relate to hormones and breeding. The weasel, which is closely related to the stoat, changes colour less dramatically in the British Isles although it does show a number of colour variations and does turn white in some other countries (Harrison Matthews).

Moulting is not essential for colour change. There are several other circumstances when this occurs. In the red squirrel the same individual hair in the coat can undergo change from red or black to white (M Shorten). The age of an animal can affect its hair colour. Young animals can have a different coat colour to adults, for example the fox cub is chocolate-brown whilst the adult is more often yellow-brown or red but the grey coat colour of the badger cub is more like that of the adult. The colour of hair can become greyer as age increases and the melanin concentration reduces.

swns.com

Most birds moult at least once a year, often about the time of breeding. But the time of moult can also be influenced by such factors as migration.

Karen Jack

Colours may also vary between males and females and some have an eclipse (masked) plumage at the end of the breeding season and may have a period in the moult when they cannot fly (I Newton).

Cold-blooded animals such as reptiles and amphibians shed the skin. In snakes before shedding, the skin becomes quite dull. Fluid gathers between the old and new layers including the scale over the eye which becomes opaque. At this time the snake becomes practically blind. Just before shedding, the eye becomes clear again as the fluid between the skin layers is reabsorbed. Shedding can occur several times a year in both amphibians and reptiles and is controlled by the thyroid gland (T Beebee and R Griffiths, 2000). The first moult occurs in the early spring when the colours can be very striking, like that of the male sand lizard which appears bright green and the male adder which often appears grey with the distinct jet black zigzag stripe down its back. Sloughing appears to promote chemical communication and brings about an increase in mating activity, especially obvious in males (Beebee and Griffiths).

Neoteny is seen in newts, especially the smooth newt. This is a condition in which the larval stage is prolonged, perhaps for years. Sometimes the colour of the neotenous form is very pale, resembling partial albino and varies in colour from cream to yellow above and white below.

Albinism, Leucism, Erythrism, Melanism and more typical varieties

Badger watching is always fascinating. There is always an element of surprise when the badger first shows at the sett entrance revealing those striking black and white facial stripes. So it is quite startling to see an albino badger appear, its head all white and with no apparent stripes. Albinos are rare and can only be found in a few counties and then in only a few localities.

The badger has a double coat of hairs which is especially obvious on the back. Here the longer guard hairs are off-white at both ends with a black bar near the tip, giving the animal a greyish overall body colour; the softer inner coat is shorter and more biscuity coloured. The facial stripes are comprised of short hairs.

The true albino badger lacks any of the pigment melanin and so is white. The albino has a pink nose, white claws, no facial stripes and the hair on the back, sides and undercarriage appears white. The eyes are also pink as there is no pigment present in the eye, so the red of blood shows through. The red colour stems from the protein haemoglobin in the oxygen-carrying red blood cells. The pure albino badger in many ways resembles the albino ferret (domesticated polecat) which is perhaps more familiar.

Melanin-producing cells derive from two different but closely aligned areas in the embryo. Firstly there are the cells which together, as the neural tube, form the developing brain and spinal cord, parts of the eye and the nerve supplying the eye (the optic nerve). Secondly, there is a group of different cells called the neural crest which forms a distinctive area close to the neural tube: these migrate into the developing skin and so are involved in the formation of hair, feathers, claws etc. There are a number of possible issues when it comes to understanding albinism. Pure albinos are correctly described as lacking all melanin pigment. Melanin is produced when the amino acid tyrosine is acted on by the enzyme tyrosinase. Melanin fails to form in the presence of the recessive gene for albinism which blocks the action of tyrosinase. This stops all melanin production in the body, whether eumelanin or pheomelanin and whatever the origin of the melanin-producing cells and wherever they happen to be found. So this includes all parts of the eye including iris and retina as well as the skin, hair, claws etc. The result is pure albinism.

One field study in Dorset began soon after a lady had discovered a badger lying up under a hedge in her garden. The lady attempted to feed the animal, an unusual coloured animal, but realising it was clearly ailing, she called in her veterinary surgeon. Unfortunately the badger died shortly afterwards. This did provide a good opportunity to examine the animal closely. The badger was an adult boar and judging by its general appearance and worn teeth was regarded as an old animal. It had a severe flank injury and appeared to have been involved in a road traffic accident. It had no evidence of any eye stripes and its head was white all over. The eyes, nose and paws were pink – coloured and its claws were long and white. The body fur had an uneven distribution of somewhat yellowish hair, particularly around the hindquarters, but the guard hairs had no coloured band in them. The yellowish colour may be the result of staining by the sand in which the setts were excavated. It was concluded this animal was a pure albino.

A thorough search for setts in the locality of the ill-fated albino badger was then undertaken. Several local landowners were approached and one local farmer produced a photograph showing badgers, including an albino. These badgers had been attracted to food put out near the house, only a short distance from one particular sett. Other setts were also found, all in close proximity, but in different habitats including a hedgerow, fields, and a copse. These setts, which were watched over a period of years, appeared to be used by one social group of badgers. Sometimes all the setts were in use with fewer badgers occupying each sett and then on other occasions one particular sett would be favoured when all the badgers were gathered together. Altogether there appeared to be between twelve and fifteen animals in this social group.

When watching badgers in this group it was also apparent that some individuals had visible evidence of facial stripes and a body colour which was more creamy in appearance, along with pink eyes, nose etc. Other individuals had slightly redder bodies and facial stripes colouration along with pink eyes and browner noses. About 40% of this group of some twelve individuals were not of the normal colouring. This seems to be more than one might expect if only a simple recessive gene for albinism was present (see below). It was concluded that there were pure albino badgers living alongside 'partial albinos' and normal-coloured badgers and that more than one recessive gene was involved. It has been suggested that the partial albinos could be described as 'eumelanistic albinos' in which some but not all melanin production was blocked. None of these colour varieties resembled the more typical erythristic badgers which have been seen in the Midlands and elsewhere.

Albinism is also known to occur in some other British wild animals. In albino hedgehogs the absence of melanin includes the spines as well as the other parts of its body. In grey squirrels, albinos are also recorded, especially from the Home Counties. At least one albino otter has been recorded in Scotland.

Leucism is a colour variation which is sometimes confused with albinism. In albinism the absence of tyrosinase activity prevents melanin production whatever the origin of melanin-producing cells. In contrast, leucism is caused by another recessive gene which occurs in populations of various animal species. Leucistic animals appear white, having both a white skin and white hair but they retain pigment colouration in the eyes. The leucistic animal does not have any black hair and the leucistic bird has white feathers.

The origins of the different pigment producing cells may still be relevant to understanding colour variations including albinism and leucism, but there are differences of opinion about this. Almost all cells which produce melanin migrate to the skin from a small raised area (the neural crest) close to but separate from where the embryonic brain is developing. The exceptions are those which also originate in the embryo but from the part which will form the brain and spinal cord (the neural tube). The melanin-producing cells originating from the neural crest in the embryo are made ineffective in leucism so the skin, hair etc. appears white. The cells which originate from the neural tube in the embryo are not involved, so the retina remains pigmented. The alternative argument is that in leucism there are no pigment cells in the skin anyway but that they are present in the eye which is not involved in the condition.

Deer provide a good example where leucism occurs. But in this case one needs to confirm skin colour as well as hair colour for confirmation. The eyes will be pigmented but there will be no black hair.

Partial leucism can occur if some melanin producing cells fail to reach for example all the skin in which case there will be patches of white hair amongst the normal-coloured hair. The piebald animal would be an example of partial leucism.

The erythristic badger fails to produce the black eumelanin and only the pheomelanin producing red pigment is apparent. The red pigment is seen most obviously in the facial stripes, the guard hairs on the back and the belly fur and legs; the eyes may appear red rather than pink. In fact the badger has a gingery appearance.

The overall sparse occurrence of erythristic badgers again suggests that this condition is due to a recessive gene, with a local distribution of carrier animals somewhat like the albino carrier with its recessive gene. Again, like the albino, the erythristic badger remains rare. Several may be seen in particular localities along with the more abundant normal-coloured individuals. There is some variation in the degree of redness in the colouration.

If the amount of melanin is abundant then another colour type of badger arises – the melanistic variety, in which the coat is particularly black but the white stripes are retained in the absence of melanocytes. This is very rare indeed, unless it has been overlooked. Badgers are occasionally found in which the black is replaced by dark brown. So there are plenty of variations once one starts looking.

Melanism can occur across a whole range of other animal types. Amongst insects it is well known in the peppered moth. Over most of its range this moth is not melanistic and is white with a variable number of black patches, streaks and spots. But the melanistic variety has black wings and therefore better camouflage in industrial areas which has helped it survive the attentions of insect-eating birds. The more usual white variety is more secure in rural areas. The reduction of industrial pollution in more recent years is likely to produce a reduction in the numbers of melanistic forms. Melanism is also recognised in the grey squirrel in North America where this animal originated.

'Blackbody radiation' is a physical characteristic, which enables the sun to be used as a source of energy more efficiently. Its significance can be illustrated in a number of wild animals. Black rabbits, for example, are found in some parts of the country along with the usual brown (agouti) ones. Taking advantage of blackbody radiation which means that heat is more readily taken up into the body than with other colours, the black ones spend less time underground and are able to spend more time feeding but consequently are susceptible to predation (R J Berry).

Black adders in which the melanism is the result of a recessive gene are particularly well known but this colour variation comes with advantages and disadvantages. The principles of blackbody radiation again apply, so basking is more efficient than in normal-coloured adders. The disadvantage is that the black adder is usually less well camouflaged and subsequently it can fall prey quite easily. But the continuing survival of black adders suggests that the advantages of being black outweigh the disadvantages. Amongst other reptiles in which melanism occurs is the smooth snake, our rarest reptile, and so it is fascinating to find that black smooth snakes can be found in one or two places in the lowland heaths of Dorset and perhaps elsewhere, along with normal-coloured ones.

In contrast, some cold-blooded animals are white because of other cell type defects and do not lack melanin. Normal metabolism can be affected in reptiles and amphibians too resulting in the absence of red and yellow pteridine pigments (pteridine is named after the Greek *pteron*, meaning wing-like, because of its double cyclic chemical structure).

Black can also be the usual colour. This applies to the European mole which has a short black velvety coat. The animal is only seen occasionally but gives itself away as it leaves telltale heaps of soil on the surface when burrowing. There are several reports of albino moles, rarely seen because of the mole's subterranean life style. The black rat, now rare, another example where the colour is usually black, can have a more variable coat clout and so can resemble the brown rat and vice versa. This can be confusing. A recessive gene appears to be involved in the melanistic variety of the brown rat.

The mink was introduced from North America and kept in fur farms. Selective breeding led to the production of several distinctive colour varieties that were popular in the fur trade. Many mink escaped or were released and a feral population still thrives in some areas along our rivers and waterways but most have reverted to the original wild colour, which is dark brown.

The polecat is another interesting example where colour variations occur in the wild. This animal is known to have spread into England from its stronghold in Wales. The breeding between polecats to produce the domesticated ferret goes back many centuries. This has produced the familiar albino ferret which is one variety found in captivity along with more normal-coloured individuals. The escape of ferrets and their crossbreeding with the polecat has resulted in variations in the colour found in wild populations, especially in England, and in the emergence of the polecat ferret as a particular type. The polecat ferret tends to be a paler brown and has white across the forehead in contrast to the polecat which is a darker individual altogether and has only a small amount of white on the face, limited to that around the eyes. There are also differences in skull shape and size and fur colour between polecats and polecat ferrets even though these two animal types can interbreed. It seems, however, that over time these mixed populations, as in mink, will revert to those with the wild type characteristics.

One of our rare mammals, the pine marten, also shows some seasonal colour variations. This mammal, another of the *mustelids*, with its characteristic creamy-yellow throat patch and white-edged ears, otherwise has a chocolate-coloured coat on its back and sides (milk chocolate in winter and plain chocolate in summer) along with black legs and facial markings, and the distinctive bushy tail.

Another rare animal, which again like the pine marten is found more especially in the Scottish Highlands, is the wildcat. This is an elusive animal whose normal markings superficially resemble the domesticated 'tabby' cat. Unfortunately crossbreeding between the wild and domesticated cat does occur but the markings of the wildcat are distinctive. Any quest to photograph the wildcat can be complicated. In his excursions into Scotland Derek Warren photographed two white kittens emerging from a badger sett, a Kellas cat, which is all black, and also the wildcat itself.

Dominant and Recessive Genes

Major advances have been made in the identification of the chemical make-up of the different types of individual cells in the various tissues of the body. There is also now more knowledge about the role of the various cell components and at the chemical level comes a greater understanding of the proteins, peptides and amino acids which make up the genes, and how these relate to DNA, RNA and other components.

Cells comprise cytoplasm inside a thin membrane and these, with the cell nucleus, form the protoplasm. The cell nucleus contains the chromosomes on which the paired genes are found. Each species has a specified number of chromosomes, each with many thousands of genes. DNA, the actual hereditary material in the genes, directs the formation of the proteins which make up each individual (R J Berry). Cells come in many forms and with special functions. Amongst these are the germ cells or gametes. It is the union of the two gamete cells, i.e. the sperm and ovum, at fertilisation which produces the single cell called a zygote which then through multiplication leads on to the development of the embryo with all its different organs and tissues.

The various colour variations under discussion here arise as a result of the action of some of these genes. The gene producing the black colouration in the coat of the badger is dominant when present. The gene responsible for albinism is recessive and unable to express itself in the presence of the dominant gene producing the black colouration in the badger's coat.

The badger is territorial and research has shown it is unusual for badgers to move over large distances. This largely restricted movement increases the likelihood of breeding between more closely related individuals. If genetic 'mutations' have occurred before, more animals with the unusual genetic makeup are likely to be present in the local population so increasing the opportunity for the mutation to show. In a population of badgers, which over a period of time has produced albinos, there will normally be several animals with the normal colour and a few which are albinos. Some of the animals of normal colour, as well as the albinos, will carry the recessive gene for albinism.

It is common to represent the dominant gene for normal colouration by the letter 'A' and use 'a' for the recessive gene for albinism. Normally genes occur in pairs. In this badger population there will be individuals which are 'AA' and 'aa' for this colouration, one normal and the other albino and a third type, Aa. These comprise three genotypes. As the Aa individual has the dominant gene A it will also look like an individual which is AA for this condition. Looking the same, these two individuals, AA and Aa, are said to have the same phenotype but are different genotypes. In a different definition, for any particular genetic condition, when the pair of genes is the same, the animal is a homozygote for that condition and when the pair of genes is different we have a heterozygote for that same condition.

Reproduction and fertilisation is very relevant when considering inheritance. If genes still occurred in pairs in each of the germ cells those in the fertilised egg; i.e. after union of sperm and egg, would be double the normal. To avoid this, the chromosomes are halved when the germ cells are produced in the gonads in the process known as meiosis.

Meiosis is the process of cell division in the gonads which results in the gametes (whether sperm or egg) each having half the number of chromosomes of the parent. At the time of fertilisation the number of chromosomes is once again restored to the original number. Unlike other chromosomes, the male and female chromosomes are very different and it is possible for some characteristics in the resulting offspring to be sex-linked. Meiosis is also an important process in which mutations can occur and enable the process of natural selection of individuals in a population to occur.

Meiosis provides the opportunity at fertilisation (of the egg by the sperm) for the embryo to have the pair of colour genes 'AA', 'Aa' or 'aa'. Only one of these three individuals will be albino ('aa') as the other two have the dominant 'A' gene present.

Tables: Mating between Animals involving the Albino recessive gene

In the tables below, illustrating the dominant 'A' gene and recessive 'a' gene, if the two animals which mate are AA and aa all the offspring will be Aa and of normal colour. If both the animals are aa, then the offspring will also be aa. If the two animals which mate are Aa, the ratio of offspring will be AA, aa and two Aa; i.e. three of normal colour and one albino.

Individual	AA	aa
Germ cells	A or A	a or a
	Fertilisation	
Offspring	Aa	

Individual	Aa	aa
Germ cells	a or a	a or a
	Fertilisation	
Offspring	Aa	

Individual	Aa	Aa
Germ cells	A or a	A or a
	Fertilisation	
Offspring	AA 2Aa aa	

Breeding programmes in various animals in captivity have shown a considerable number of colour variations within particular species which otherwise would almost certainly not have been identified in wild populations. Some of the colour variations include albino rats, mice and rabbits amongst others. Such programmes have helped in the understanding of the science, including genetics, involved. These studies, however revealing, would not normally be possible using free-living wild animals. It remains for naturalists to study and record the differences within the various species of wild animal that they encounter and so contribute to our understanding.

Bibliography

Anderson, S. (1990) *Seals,* Whittet Books.

Ashby, E. (2000) *My Life with Foxes,*Robert Hale.

Birks, J. (2002) *The Pine Marten,* Mammal Society, Species Series

Bright, P. & Morris, P. (2005) *The Dormouse,* Mammal Society, Species Series.

Burness, G. (1970) *The White Badger,* London: Harrap.

Burrows, R. (1968) *Wild Fox,* David & Charles.

Chanin, P. (1985) *The Natural History of Otters,* Croom Helm.

Chanin, P. (2013) *Otters, The British Natural History Collection* Whittet Books.

Clark, M. (1981) *Mammal Watching,* Severn House.

Drabble, P. (1979) *No Badgers In My Wood,* Michael Joseph.

Evans, G. & Thomson, D.(1972) *The Leaping Hare,* Faber & Faber

Gorman, L. & Stone, D. (1990) *Moles,* Christopher Helm.

Gurnell, J. Lutz, P. & Wauters, L. *Squirrels,* Mammal Society.

Harris, S. & Yalden, D. (2008) *Mammals of the British Isles,* Handbook. 4th Edition. The Mammal Society.

Harris, S. (1986) *Urban Foxes,* Whittet Books.

Harris, S. (1979) *The Secret Life of the Harvest Mouse, Hamyln.*

Herter, K. (1963) *Hedgehogs,* Phoenix House

Hill, J. & Smith, J. (1984) *Bats: A Natural History,* British Museum.

Holm, J. (1987) *Squirrels,* Whittet Books.

Kolb, H. (1996) *Country Foxes,* Whittet Books.

Kruuk, H. & Parish, T. (1997) *Behaviour of Badgers,* Institute of Terrestial Ecology, Natural Environment Research Council.

Kruuk, H. (1989) *The Social Badger,* Oxford University Press.

Kruuk, H. (1995) *Wild Otters,* Oxford University Press.

Laidler, K. (1980) *Squirrels in Britain,* David and Charles.

Lawrence, M. J. & Brown, R. W. (1967) *Mammals of Britain,* Blandford Press.

Lockley, R. (1964) *The Private Life of The Rabbit,* Andre Deutsh.

Lovegrove, R. (2007) *Silent Fields,* Oxford University Press.

Lloyd, H. G. (1980) *The Red Fox,* Batsford.

Marquiss, R. (1987) et al. *The Nature of Nottinghamshire,* Barracuda Books.

Matthews, L. H. (1982) *Mammals in the British Isles,* Collins.

Macdonald, D. (1987) *Running with the Fox,* Unwin Hymen.

McDonald, R. & Harris, S. (1997) *Stoats and Weasels,* Mammal Society, Species Series.

Mallon, D. (2001) *The Mountain Hare in the Peak District,* Derbyshire Wildlife Trust.

Morris, P. (2011) *Dormice,* Whittet Books.

Morris, P. (2010) *The Hedgehog,* Mammal Society, Special Series.

Morris, P. (2014) *Hedgehogs,* Whittet Books.

Neal, E. (1948) *The Badger,* The New Naturalist, Collins.

Neal, E. & Cheeseman C. (1996) *Badgers,* Poyser.

Neal, E. (1986) *The Natural History of Badgers,* Croom Helm.

Neal, E. (1997) *Badgers,* Blandford Press.

Neal, E. (1994) *The Badger Man, Memoirs of a Biologist,* Providence Press.

Paget,R.J. and Middleton, A. (1974) *Badgers of Yorkshire and Humberside,* Sessions of York.

Pearce, G. (2010) *Badger Behaviour, Conservation & Rehabilitation,* Pelagic Publications.

Ratcliffe, E.J. (1974) *Through the Badger Gate,* G. Bell & Sons.

Roper, T.J. (2010) *Badgers,* Collins.

Schober, W. & Grimmberger, E. (1987) *A Guide to Bats Of Britain & Europe,* Hamlyn.

Sleeman, P. (1989) *Stoats & Weasels-Polecats & Martens,* Whittet Books.

Tapper, S. & Yalden, D. (2010) *The Brown Hare,* Mammal Society.

Tittensor, A. (1980) *The Red Squirrel,* Mammal Society Series, Blandford.

Tomkies, M. (1991) *Wildcats,* Whittet Books.

Twigg, G. (1975) *The Brown Rat,* David & Charles.

Waters, D. & Warren, R. (2009) *Bats,* Mammal Society, Species Series.

Woods, M. (2010) *The Badger,* Mammal Society, Species Series.